DEANNE FITZPATRICK

SIMPLY MODERN

Contemporary Designs
for Hooked Rugs

NIMBUS
PUBLISHING
nimbus.ca

Nimbus Publishing Limited
3731 Mackintosh St, Halifax, NS   B3K 5A5
(902) 455-4286 nimbus.ca
Printed and bound in Canada
NB1150

Cover and Interior design: Kate Westphal, Graphic Detail
Photography by Catherine Bussiere and Mike Tompkins

Library and Archives Canada Cataloguing in Publication

Fitzpatrick, Deanne, author
Simply modern : contemporary design for hooked rugs /
Deanne Fitzpatrick.
Includes index.
Issued in print and electronic formats.
ISBN 978-1-77108-216-7 (bound).—ISBN 978-1-77108-217-4 (html)

1. Rugs, Hooked. I. Title.
TT850.F584 2014   746.7'4   C2014-903203-X
                                                     C2014-903204-8

Nimbus Publishing acknowledges the financial support for its publishing activities from the Government of Canada through the Canada Book Fund (CBF) and the Canada Council for the Arts, and from the Province of Nova Scotia through Film & Creative Industries Nova Scotia. We are pleased to work in partnership with Film & Creative Industries Nova Scotia to develop and promote our creative industries for the benefit of all Nova Scotians.

*Dedicated to the lovely
women who work with me in
my studio, day in, day out:
you do so much for me.*

CONTENTS

INTRODUCTION

When my mother started hooking rugs again after a sixty-five-year break, she wanted to hook stripes. At the time, to me, it seemed old-fashioned. My mother had hooked rugs for her mother as a little one around the house. It must have been one of her fonder memories, I think, for she talked very little about her childhood to me. She had a few stories that she would re-tell if I asked her. One of her favourites was about salting fish "up on the Labrador," as she referred to it, with her father. After I began hooking rugs she would also tell me about making mats with her mother. Her stories were simple and steady, and varied little between tellings. She never embellished things much.

I wanted to know more, of course, but she had little to tell or was unwilling; I was never sure which. Once I began hooking mats, though, my mother's interest was sparked. She thought I was foolish to consider the idea of making a living from it, and giving up a good job, but nonetheless, she was curious enough to go at it again after a sixty-five-year break. And when she did, it was stripes that she wanted to hook. No matter what design I drew on the burlap for her, she would find a way to stripe it.

Now, nearly twenty years later, I think that some of my mother's sense of simplicity has sunk in. I too am interested in stripes and squares, circles and other simple shapes. It started for me with a series of commissioned rugs I did for an interior designer about five years ago. At first, recreating the traditional designs did not really appeal to me. The interior designer had a client who wanted a series of very simple old-fashioned geometric designs, and the family had suggested she see if I could do them. They sent me some colour swatches and I set to work on creating a series of rugs much like the ones my grandmothers or my mother would have made. I started out thinking it would be a nice break from the designs I usually do, but at first I was not particularly excited about it. The excitement came as I hooked the rugs.

There was a peace in making these rugs, knowing they were going to be used for the floor. As I saw the colours and designs come together I became more inspired. That project got me back to the importance of simplicity when making my rugs. I am so thankful for that project because it led me somewhere new. It was not what I was looking for at the time: then I was still trying to be more narrative and tell stories with my rugs, or at least focus on a central image. But where you end up in art just because you head to the studio every day and make things is not always where you planned to go.

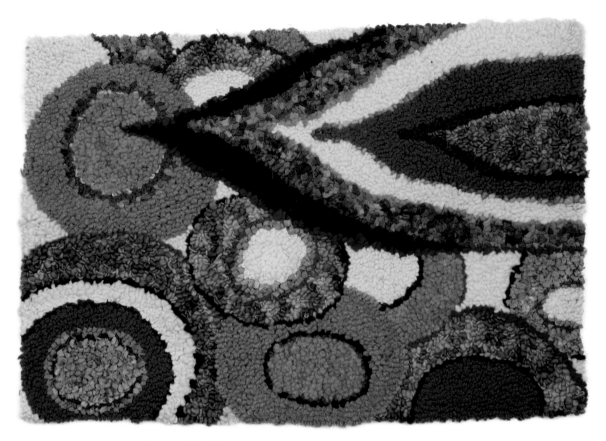

Modern leaf and hoop, 20 by 30 inches.

Cumberland Key, 15 by 16 inches.

And making those geometric mats was just another step along the road to this book. Over the years, whenever I ran short of ideas I would go back to simple designs only to find that keeping a design simple was quite a big puzzle sometimes. Yet the puzzle always intrigued me, and once I worked it out I would get lost in the hooking in a way that did not happen with some of my more pictorial designs. Often we do things for one reason only to discover that the benefit we get from it is not what we expected at all. When I started creating simple modern designs, mostly I was just taking a break from the way I had been doing things. Instead I discovered that I really enjoyed working in a new way.

I also discovered that I *could* create thoroughly modern-looking designs and that I even liked them myself. Once they started showing up, I was able to tap into a new sensibility within myself, one that gave me something in common with my mother.

Then in the winter of 2013 a young woman, Megan Ingman, started coming to our Thursday Fibre Arts Group and I liked the border of a rug that she was working on. Something in her rug, though she was just learning to hook, sparked an idea in me to play a little harder with simple designs that had a contemporary feel to them. I started making elemental shapes, and using colour to bring out the graphic nature of the shapes. Seeing these first few rugs as a departure from my more recent rugs, I decided that I wanted to keep pushing it to see where it might lead. Eventually it led to the rugs shown and the ideas I put forth in this book for you to learn from. Over the years I have always added a modern edge to my work, in that it was different from traditional rugs, but in this book I have pushed it much further and I think they feel distinctly modern. I hope you'll agree.

Cumberland Leaf, 15 by 15 inches.

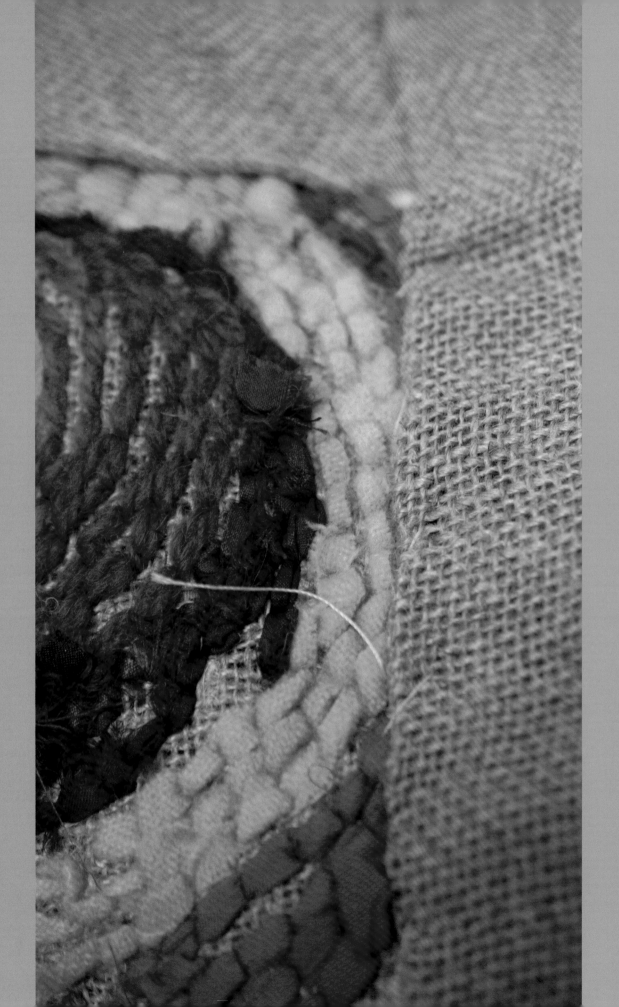

THE BASICS OF HOOKING RUGS

*T*here is only one stitch to learn—that tells you just how easy it is to hook a rug. When I first learned I thought for sure there must be some knotting or tying involved, but the woman who taught me, Marion Kennedy, insisted that it was just the one stitch. It is so simple that when I show people, their first response is often, "Is that all there is?" I laugh and say yes, and they sit down excited to learn something new.

BASIC INSTRUCTIONS

Use recycled wool cloth or new cloth and cut it into strips between 1/4 and 1/2 an inch wide. My general rule is, the thinner the fabric the wider I cut it. This works well because lightweight fabrics hook better when cut wider, while thicker fabrics are easier to pull through when they are cut narrower.

If you use a wool cutter designed for rug hooking it will define the width of your cloth strip, with 3 being the narrowest and 10 being the widest. I use numbers 6 and 8, which are around 1/4 of an inch wide. I also use a lot of hand-cut wools, which are often wider, up to 1 inch wide if the wool is thin and lightweight. It adds an interesting texture to my mats.

Choose the right backing for the wool you want to hook. I use only open-weave linen or burlap because the wools I use are often wide cuts and I want them to fit through the holes in the backing. This is important because if you're trying to pull thick cuts of cloth through narrow openings in the backing, you will wind up hurting your hand.

Attach your backing to a rug-hooking frame or hoop so that it is tight like a drum. You can also stretch it like a canvas over a stretcher frame. The main thing is that it be taut as this makes it easy to pull the cloth through. If the backing is loose you will be tugging on the hook and the cloth will not slide through the backing easily. Stretch it tight and the hook will be able to glide through.

Draw a simple design on the backing with a black marker. I use Sharpies for this because they do not bleed. Your design can be as simple as a square or a circle. If it is more complicated, just be sure to not put in too many tiny details as they will be difficult to hook using wider cuts of wool.

When you draw your pattern on, make sure you leave 4 inches of excess linen or burlap all around the outside edge as you will need this to attach your pattern to the frame.

Take a strip of wool in one hand and put your hook in your other hand. I hold my hook like I would hold a pencil.

Put your hook down through the burlap and find your hand with the wool in it on the other side. Catch the wool with your hook and bring the end of the strip up to the surface of the backing. The ends of the wool strips should be on the surface of the mat. You will then cut them off, level with the loops you hook so that they blend into the rug. You do not want to leave them on the back because it makes them easy to tear out.

After you bring the first end up, pull the strip again and it will form a loop. Keep hooking loop by loop, skipping lots of holes. You want to make sure that the surface of your rug is covered with loops but you do not want to hook too tightly because if you do, your rug will not lie flat.

Skip every second or third hole, depending on the width and thickness of both the fabric you are hooking and the weave of your backing. You will know. From the top side of your rug you should not be able to see any burlap. From the back side of your rug you will be able to see some thin lines of burlap and that is fine.

Traditionally in rug hooking you outline the drawing of your design and then fill in the area. You can start anywhere on the rug, but most people start by outlining and then filling in.

You do not have to hook in any special way such as straight lines or curly lines. I change the direction of my hooking depending on what I am hooking. This means I hook in all different directions using all kinds of motions.

When you finish a strip, make sure you bring the end to the surface. The rug is created by the packing of the loops together and blending in the ends so you cannot see them. The natural weave of the backing that opens and closes as you pull the loops through keeps the loops secure and in place.

When the whole surface is hooked you have completed your rug!

I bind my rugs by cutting away all but 2 inches of the excess burlap around the design. I then fold the excess burlap twice so that all the raw edges are folded in and I hand-sew the burlap to the back of the rug using a hem stitch.

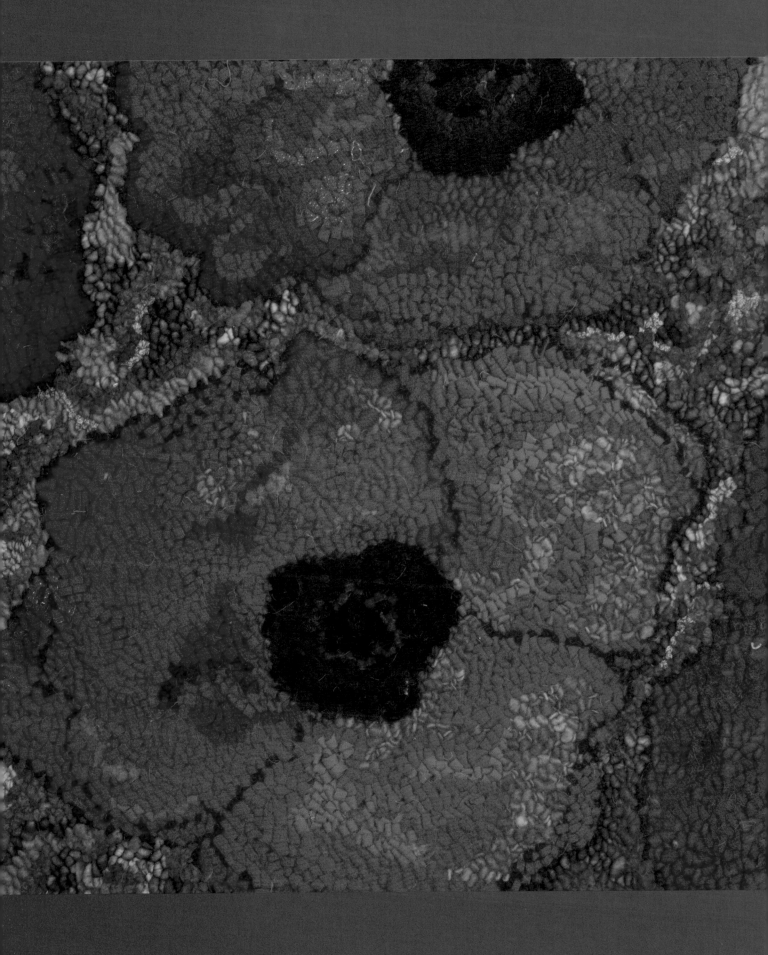

CHAPTER ONE

A MODERN APPROACH

My mother could never pronounce the word modern. Instead she would say "modren." When I was a kid and discovered the real pronunciation of the word I remember thinking my mother was backward, the way kids sometimes do. I'd feel really bad about that, except now I hear my own children mocking the way I say words. We mothers know it and accept it. We grow out of it.

So the idea of modern came to me gradually. I lived in a very traditional Irish Catholic community in rural Newfoundland and anything modern, or even modren, seemed to be outside of our lives. I looked to the Americans at the navy base in Argentia, or to my aunt who lived in St. John's, or to my sisters who had moved to the mainland to define for me what was modern. I had no idea that over time I would come to see simplicity and modernity in the same light.

The idea of modern or contemporary is an odd one, when you think about it, because what is modern to one person is not to another. It depends on your time and place. What was modern to my mother was plastic. She loved plastic. I don't like plastic because it seems old-fashioned to me. Modern is about what is new and contemporary in *your* life. I believe there is a personal perspective to what we perceive as modern. What is fresh and new and sleek to one person may not be to another. Right now I see what I once saw as old-fashioned as modern. This is because trends and fashion change and with them our tastes.

When it comes to art, modern and contemporary tend to mean different things. The terms "Modern" and "Postmodern" typically cover artwork created between the 1860s and the 1970s. Modern art was considered to include work that was experimental and fresh, and began with painters such as Van Gogh, Cézanne, and Seurat. Contemporary art is generally seen as work produced in the present time, though since the early 1900s there have been Contemporary Art societies throughout the world. Contemporary art simply means art *of* the time it was made, whether that was in the 1900's or the present day. Though I also believe that when you say "contemporary art," the connotation is that it is of modern design. So you can see it can get to be a bit confusing. What is modern? What is contemporary? I'd say there are some general guidelines with lots of room for movement and your definition probably varies with your experience. So we begin this book with an ill-defined understanding, and a need to sort out our own definition.

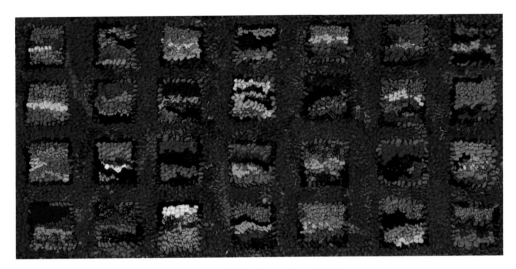

Tiny Landscapes. The little squares framed in this rug were inspired by a modern quilt I had seen.

In terms of hooked mats, I think these terms, "contemporary" or "modern" have become different again. For the purposes of this book I would like to use the term "modern" to explain that these rugs, though they use the same method as more traditional rugs, offer a fresh sense of design. They are original, and though inspired by tradition, they are not hanging on to it. The designs I have created for this book are contemporary in that they reflect my world now. I live in a different place than my grandmother and even my mother did when they hooked their rugs. In fact, the world has changed immensely since I first began hooking rugs. Twenty-two years ago, there was very little technology in the home. Since I began hooking rugs, personal computers have become part of our daily life. The Internet has revolutionized the way we communicate and what we can see and understand at a moment's notice. I remember sitting my son on my knee when we got our first home computer years ago, not knowing that this tool in front of us was about to revolutionize us all.

This contemporary place where I belong now is one where heads are bent over iPads and computers rather than mat frames. It is a place where images are everywhere and attention spans are short. This world is full of things trying to grab our attention. This access to facts and ideas may be one of the most profound differences between our present generation and those of previous mat hookers. And we see so much more in terms of design. We are not limited to what we saw at our neighbour's house, or in the mail-order catalogue. The world of design is a few clicks away, we can see thousands of images of anything within a few seconds. We can explore trends and artists from across the globe. All our work is susceptible to extraordinary influences to a degree that artists have never had to deal with before.

My grandmother on the other hand, when she was hooking rugs, had never been farther than perhaps a hundred miles from her home. Printed materials were a luxury. She found inspiration in very little outside of her daily life. Perhaps there were a few signs advertising goods at the local merchant's, prints on fabrics, and children's schoolbooks. Today design is everywhere. From the bite out of the apple on our iPods and laptops, to tomato cans, to magazines, we are constantly influenced by the way other people see things. We are constantly reminded of other people's sensibilities.

As interesting as this can make our world, it can also be overwhelming. It can interfere with figuring out just what our own sensibilities are. We see so much it is hard to distinguish between what we really love and what catches our eye. Having something catch our eye is very different from finding something truly beautiful and being inspired by it. We have a lot more opportunity *and* a lot more to sort through as we create designs for hooked mats.

Some of course wonder whether hooked mats can even be considered art, let alone contemporary or modern art. I believe that anything can be art if it is made with the spirit of an artist. I think it is not the thing itself that defines whether or not something can be art, but how it was made. For me, if the design is original and if it is inspired by the creativity of the person who made it, then almost anything can be art. This statement of course does not really define which hooked rugs are considered art. This is up to the viewer, I suppose. But rug hooking is just a medium like any other, and making art is not so much about what you do but how you do it.

Modern Lifestyle: Rugs in the Home

Hooked rugs can live in any home. They are versatile, strong, and beautiful. It is really the design of the hooked rug that makes it feel as if it belongs (or not). I think there is a misconception that hooked rugs are always folksy or antique reproductions, and they can be those things, but I also believe that with the right design and mounting, a hooked rug can add a very modern element to the home.

Textiles such as rugs, spreads, and pillows soften the home, making it a place to settle. My first house is the house I still live in. I moved into it when I was twenty-four. I had no money but I had ideas and dreams for the place. There were four rooms over four rooms—eight empty rooms for me to re-imagine. I remember wandering around them thinking that they would never be filled. The farmhouse, as it was then, was austere, and I felt a kind of love for it. It was the love of the possibilities ahead. When I look back at those empty rooms I still feel that initial wonder. Twenty-three years later nearly every room has had a life or two of its own. Of course the filling came easy, and at times the rooms overflowed in farmhouse style.

Rugs have many uses. The main one, though, is to add comfort and warmth to our lives.

One of the things I filled the house with was hooked mats. In fact it was the house that led me to hooking. The big wide floorboards seemed to call out for old-style hooked rugs. I followed the lead of the house and ended up becoming an artist and hooking rugs every day. We moved in the fall of 1990, right around the time I graduated with a masters degree in counselling, and the same fall I learned how to hook rugs. For a while I was betwixt and between, but it was only a few years before I left the counselling behind altogether. I was pulled towards making mats in a way that I cannot explain. It was forceful and in the end I just gave in to it.

Through the years the eight rooms in my house have expanded to eleven as we renovated the old back kitchen and loft. They have seen lots of reinventions, changing usages and styles as the needs of my family evolved and as my tastes changed with the times.

In the last few years I've tired a little of the country farmhouse feeling and have moved towards a sparser style. It's not a sleek modern, but more of a country modern. As my children have grown in the house and now are closer to moving out, the rooms feel bigger again. There is room to move without Lego underfoot. In my own home I have come to feel that it is perfectly alright to be eclectic. I respect the farmhouse bones of the place but if I feel like a more modern painting or piece of furniture, then by all means, I add it freely. I like the mix of the modern with the farmhouse and it works for my lifestyle.

I feel the same way about hooked rugs. I respect the longstanding tradition of mat making but I do not think I have to hold fast to that tradition. I love the idea of mats hooked on burlap bags from a family's woolen clothes, but honestly that tradition is from another time when our food came in feed sacks, and we wore woolen pants, shirts, and skirts. There is no way I can hold on to the purity of that tradition and still encourage people to hook rugs. I need to be open about materials in order to continue to ensure that rug hooking has an interesting and viable future. Just like years ago, when women first started hooking rugs to warm drafty floors, we have to use what we have. The materials we have access to are what we need to hook with. Wool, thankfully, is still accessible, as are many interesting yarns.

In terms of design the tradition was to make mats for the floor. Rugs were designed to emulate the imported carpets contained in the homes of merchants and the families that could afford them. A woman working in service in a home would see these fine imported carpets and would try to recreate similar designs for her hooked mats.

Rugs lived on the floor, so the designs were created to be looked down at. Of course these things affect the elements and evolution of traditional rug design. These rugs often had scrolls in the four corners and flowers in the centre. In 1990, Doreen Wright and Nanette Ryan compiled a wonderful book called *Garretts and the Bluenose Rugs of Nova Scotia* which catalogues many of the traditional rug-hooking patterns that

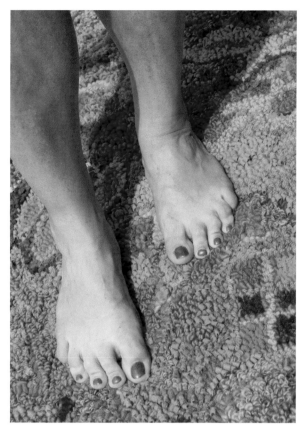

May we never get so modern about hooked rugs that we forget how beautiful they are underfoot.

Garrett's sold starting in the 1920s. Garrett's of New Glasgow, Nova Scotia, were well known for the rug-pattern business and sold their Bluenose Rug Hooking patterns all over North America. At the height of their business they were importing 150,000 yards of burlap from Scotland each year. The patterns were almost all floral and scrollwork, considered the most traditional of rug-hooking designs.

I respect these designs. They remain lovely. Though in terms of taste and style I have found that even though I live in a house that was probably once filled with these kinds of rugs, my preferences have changed. When we first bought the house twenty-five years ago, it was these traditional mats that I sought out, but I find I am interested in more modern and contemporary designs now, both in terms of what I want to hook and what I want to live with.

Rug hooking as medium is not in itself only good for traditional designs. It has wonderful possibilities for modern design and inspiration. The technique is just a tool to create rugs for your home that speak of now and suit your personal lifestyle and home style. Whether your home has old farmhouse bones or a strong urban and modern style, hooked rugs can be part of the design or decor because the materials and colours used together with the design define the rug: rug hooking itself is not the style.

A Mindful Craft

Every couple of years I try to meditate again. I really like the idea of it, but the truth is I never have much success. Sometimes I do it faithfully for weeks at a time, but then slowly it slips away from me. When this happens I remind myself that thrumming of the hook might be my mantra. If you sit for hours at a time with a craft such as rug hooking, quilting, or knitting, you really do get to a meditative state. The craft is a kind of meditation in itself.

Years ago, people often referred to these crafts as mindless. I think I might have thought of them that way myself, believing that you really did not have to think about them as you did them. They were seen as a way to pass the time, relegated to people who had lots of it. Needless to say, my views on the nature of craft, and so have the views of many others.

Mihaly Csikszentmihalyi's idea of flow is widely accepted in psychology. Flow is about being fully immersed in an activity, focused and enjoying it to the point that you no longer notice time. It is the idea of getting "in the zone" as you work with single-mindedness on a craft. It is why we love to make things, because in doing so we are lost in time. We get immersed in the beauty of wool, the silkiness of yarn. Being in a state of flow is seen as being focused entirely upon and concentrating on the present moment so that your awareness and your actions become one. Csikszentmihalyi created this concept based on his research with artists who, upon getting lost in their work, would forget about basic personal needs such as food, water, or even sleep.

With the emerging focus on and value placed upon being in the present moment and being aware of your emotions, your body, your feelings, and your surroundings, I also understand rug hooking as a practice in mindfulness. This is different from the idea of flow, in which time passes unbeknownst to us and we slip into a state of being lost in our work. Rug hooking can be a practice of mindfulness as well, as we remain aware of every stitch, and every colour, each loop pulled in a rhythm.

Whether you see craft as something that is mindful or mindless, either experience can be a comfort. There are times when you need to let your mind wander and think whatever it wants to think. This is an important part of creativity. Other times it may be important to try to focus your mind on the moment or the task at hand, rather than letting it wander. In my experience, both are necessary. Rug hooking helps me with both and I think this in itself makes it a modern-day craft. It is a retreat from media, computers, and technology in general, at a time when this retreat is much needed. We live in a world where many of us need to find a way to get back to ourselves and the simple things in life, and rug hooking can be a pathway to that.

When I think of modern design for hooked rugs, it means a movement away from the heavy outlining of houses, animals, and traditional designs with central medallions and decorations in the corners, and towards a more modern sensibility. In this book I use a lot of strong graphic designs, bold colours, and some abstract designs. The bold florals you'll find here as well as the landscapes are clearly identifiable, but they are very different from the approach to imagery you find in traditional hooked rugs.

Tea and Roses, 24 by 24 inches.

CHAPTER TWO

BASICS OF DESIGN

G reat design is something you know when you see it. One of the ways of learning how to create good rug designs is by evaluating what you see and examining why you believe it to be good design. What do you like about it?

I look everywhere for good design, from matchbooks, to the labels on packaging, to paintings. Design ideas are abundant, and as you begin or continue to design your own rugs you will find that you constantly run into new design possibilities. Once you start looking for design ideas the real challenge will be the one we discussed earlier: to filter all these ideas and narrow in on the ones that really speak to you and that work for the medium of rug hooking.

BASIC DESIGN TOOLS FOR RUG HOOKING

Keep these things on hand so that they are easy to reach when you need them. These are design essentials.

- Pencils, pens
- Sketchbooks and notebooks
- Rulers, T-squares
- Templates or patterns
- Red dot tracer
- Wedding tulle
- Sharpie markers
- Backings of burlap or linen that have been serged or taped to prevent fraying

The first thing is making sure you have the basic tools ready.

Next are levels of design. I like to think there are two levels of design in creating hooked rugs. The first level (A) involves working with simple shapes, and the second (B) ventures more into self-expression. I do not think that one level necessarily has to come before the other, but it is often more comfortable for someone to begin by starting with a simple shape.

Either level of design is fine, and you'll know where you should start. Design is not so much about drawing freehand as it is about putting elements of the rug together and using colours and textures to make it as pleasing and beautiful as it can be. Just start at the place you are at.

We are often held back from doing things because we want to be better than we already are before we start. Think about that for a second. What a great stalling tactic this is from becoming better at anything! Sometimes this is really just avoidance. You are avoiding something that you really do not want to do. Other times it is inhibition or fear. If you discover that the reason you might be having trouble getting started is inhibition, then I say jump right in. Your first pieces are just that, first pieces. They are practice pieces for you to learn on. Very few of us look back on our body of work and think our first pieces were the best. We grow and get better each time we make something.

So just get started. If you want to create great hooked rugs that reflect you, that speak of your style, then you need to begin to play with design. This can mean starting with a simple square, a diamond, a circle, or any shape, and growing from there.

Some Important Elements of Designing Hooked Rugs

When you begin designing hooked rugs there are many things to consider. It is only from actively designing that you will learn these things. As long as you keep designing rugs and finishing them, you will see your abilities progress. I have learned much more from looking at completed rugs that I felt had a flaw or a mistake than I did from pulling out and changing wools while a rug was in progress.

Sharpies are probably one of my favourite tools. Though I do like to play with markers and pencils, mostly I love the way they look in a jar.

We learn by losing our attachment to the perfect finished product and embracing the process of making for the sake of making. No rug will be perfect—even a masterpiece might have a flaw. As you begin to design consider the following.

LINE

Lines can be straight and hard, or soft and organic. Very firm straight lines in hooked rugs remind me of geometric design while soft curvy lines remind me of florals and backgrounds. You have a choice in how you hook your lines. You can hook them in swirls, circles, little boxes, or thick strokes, and the way you choose to hook your lines will have an impact on your design.

It is not only your hooked line that matters but the strength of the line that you draw for your pattern. That line can be soft or hard, and of course, as the foundation for your design, it will define what kind of line you hook.

Hooking in circular motion, or in any direction, is simply a matter of following the line drawn on the backing. There is no special technique for this.

SUBJECT MATTER

What is your rug about? Subject matter is endless. It can be realistic, surreal, abstract, narrative, organic. The real question is what is your rug about? What is the focus? This goes back to your style and what you are interested in. Sort out your ideas and pursue designing something that is relevant and that matters to you.

LEVEL A

- You can start with a simple shape such as a star or a square and repeat it and play with it.
- You can try to create an original work based on inspiration you found elsewhere.
- You can start with a photograph that someone else took.
- You can use a template or a traced image from a colouring book to create a basic design.
- You can use an overhead projector or wedding tulle to trace an enlarged design onto your backing.
- You can use templates that you trace but arrange into a design yourself.

LEVEL B

- You work straight from your head drawing right on the burlap.
- You use a photograph or image from your own experience, one that you took.
- You create the sketches for the pattern freehand.

Two Birds on the crest of a wave.

COMPOSITION

This is the organization of the elements of a work of art. You can learn more about formal rules of composition in visual art on the Internet or in a good art book, such as *Painting and Understanding Abstract Art* by John Lowry (Crowood Press, 2010) or *Conversations in Paint* by Charles Dunn (Workman, 1995). Remember, many of these principles translate from painting to rug hooking easily. Essentially, once you decide on the subject matter it is about how you lay out your image or design onto your backing.

The goal is to create a sense of wholeness throughout the mat, so that it is pleasing and interesting to the eye. You want to consider the whole area you have to work with. This does not mean that there is something occupying every space, but as a designer you need to decide where there will be activity and where the eye should rest. All the parts of the mat should work together to create a whole.

So much of composition and design is about choice. What do you leave in? What do you leave out? Which elements go where? These are important questions that only the designer can define.

SPACE, SCALE, AND SIZE

These are important elements of composition. You'll need to decide how big an image you are going to use. If the rug is about apples, is it a close-up of the core showing the seeds, or a basket of apples? Are there many apples or just one or two? Where are they placed in the design? How much space is between them? How big is the rug as a whole? What shape is the rug? Are the edges even or ragged or curvy?

COLOUR

Colour evokes feeling; choose your colours based on this. There are no rights and wrongs when it comes to colour choices but they can dramatically affect the feeling of the mat you are making.

I like to make dramatic changes in my colour palettes from rug to rug. Some artists like to work in the same palette repeatedly. What do you like? How can colour help define your style?

BALANCE

Balance is a critical element of composition. The goal of balance in a rug is to avoid making one side too heavy and the other too light. Though it is important that there be blank space or places for the eye to rest, such as background area in some rugs, it is not a good idea to have one area of your design very heavily weighted with lots of interest and activity and the other area left plain. This does not mean that everything has to be perfectly balanced, as in equally weighted, but that important parts of composition are distributed throughout the mat.

The rule of thirds, which has been around since the 1300s, supposes that a picture should be divided into nine equal parts and that the activity should happen at the intersection of these parts. It is a good rule for beginning to understand balance in composition, even if sometimes you decide you need to break it! In a rug, not only do the colour, shape, and size of the elements need to be balanced, you also need to make sure that the texture is balanced nicely throughout.

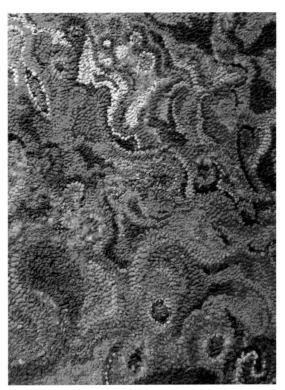

Looking at a rug up close and looking at it from a distance changes the rug completely. Step away from your work to really see it.

You can see that the back of the rug does not need to be completely filled. It is okay to see a little burlap. If you hook too tight your rugs will not lie flat and might curl.

PERSPECTIVE

Perspective in drawing and painting simply means that the closer you want the object to appear, the larger it is; if you want it to appear farther away, make it smaller. In rug design you can have perspective matter or you can simply say it does not and forget about it altogether. This is perfectly acceptable, and in fact there is a long tradition of it in rug hooking.

FOCAL POINT

As you create the design for your rug it is important to remember the value of a point of interest. This is the place where the eye is led, the part of the rug that draws the viewer in, makes them curious. Often if there are houses, trees, or people in a landscape rug, they may become the point of interest. Make sure there is some element in your rug that demands the attention of the viewer.

Simplicity in Design

"Real Goodness is always simple. Simplicity is so attractive and so profitable that it is strange that so few people are really simple." Leo Tolstoy

In a world where everything is complicated, simplicity has gained new momentum and we are now more interested in trying to understand the beauty of keeping things easy.

When I first started rug hooking it was all about simplicity for me. I wanted to use burlap bags and recycled clothing. I found the idea of dyeing wool complicated and couldn't imagine I would ever venture into it. I started out as simply as I could, and gradually, over time, things that once seemed overwhelming appeared simpler and I grew into them, learning as I went. Simplicity is about growing into things at the right pace and shedding what you no longer need or require. Keeping things simple can still happen as we grow and develop.

Simplicity is not as simple as we are led to believe. My notion of simplicity changed as my needs changed, as the world around me changed, and as I gained more knowledge. One important thing I learned is that what is simple for a person with the right tools is difficult for a person without them. A woman with a hammer can pound a nail far more easily than a woman with a shoe. Trust me: I know, having tried both ways.

One of the things that makes rug hooking modern is its simplicity. There is only one stitch to learn. You simply take a strip of wool cloth or yarn and pull it through a hole in the burlap or linen. Then you continue to pull the strip, loop by loop, until it is finished. The tools you need are fairly simple: a good hook, a frame, a nice open-weave backing, and some wool—but it is always preferable to have the best of each of these that you can afford.

You can carry this notion of simplicity into design. You can take the simplest of motifs and create very interesting rugs with them. A circle, a square, any shape can be repeated, morphed, and changed to create interesting rugs by using the design principles outlined in this chapter. What I have found is that when you take the most traditional of shapes and hook them you can end up with very modern-looking rugs. When you look at modern paintings, for example Kandinsky's *Circles*, you will often see the same thing: modern-looking design relies heavily on simple shapes and lines. We can learn from these modern paintings and find new ways to reinvent circles, squares, and other shapes and patterns into modern-looking hooked rugs.

SOME SIMPLE AND WELL-USED DESIGN RULES

- Omit or truncate: show half or part of things. Not everything needs to be shown as a whole.
- Avoid horizontal lines across the middle of the rug.
- Simplify your lines and design as much as you can.
- Use the whole space.
- The rule of thirds: in a landscape the first third is foreground, the last third is distance, the centre is middle ground.
- Use odd numbers for groupings.
- Repeat motifs and patterns.
- Turn the above rules upside down, inside out, and otherwise break them whenever necessary.

Activity: DESIGN

Take a template such as a circle or a square and recreate it in different sizes. Take some of the different sizes and fold them in halves and quarters. Use the templates to create a design. You can try this with paper in your sketchbook or you can try larger templates by designing right on your backing, depending on your confidence level. The beauty of designing in your sketchbook is that you can take your finished design, photocopy it, and work out some colour ideas with coloured pencils. If you do not make the designs on burlap too large, they can also be good for creating little studies on which to play with colour.

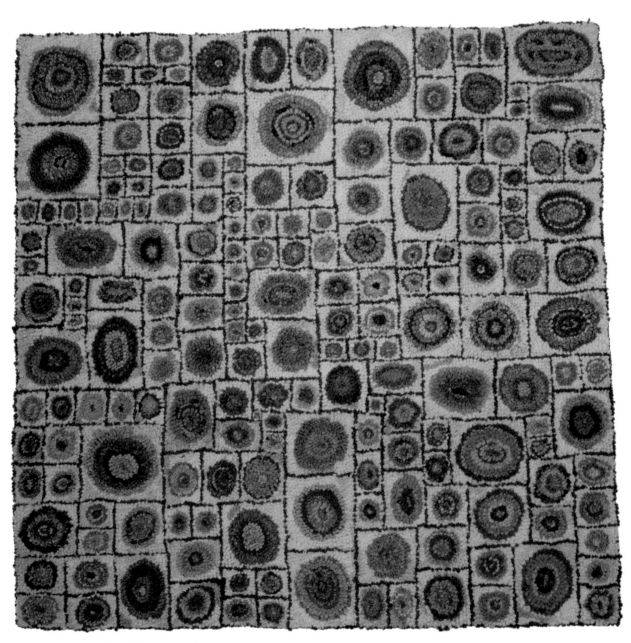

Circle Square, 52 by 53 inches.

Seven Trees, 54 by 54 inches.

4⁷/8 X 6⁷/8

CHAPTER THREE

DRAWING FOR RUG HOOKING

*D*rawing is different from design. You can design without ever having to draw, and you can draw without considering design. They are complementary of course but one is not necessary for the other. So often people have stifled ideas about their drawing abilities. When we were kids we drew freely without judgment, but as we grew older and started comparing our drawings to others' we became critical of our work and got discouraged. Most of us gave up our pencils all together. Rug hooking is a great way to get back to drawing because the kind of drawing that it requires is so simple. Also, because the drawing is not the end product, it allows us to make mistakes that can be fixed easily as we hook the design.

Though I keep sketchbooks and draw in them, when I am getting ready to hook a rug I like to draw right on the burlap or linen. I often close the sketchbook if I have made prior sketches because I find that I try to copy the sketch rather than relax into the drawing. Drawing freehand like this means I often make mistakes. But the beauty of drawing for rug hooking is that you can just turn over the backing and take a second go at it. If you mess up both sides, you can draw it again with a different coloured marker such as red or hot pink. I always use Sharpie brand markers for drawing on burlap or linen as they are permanent and never run. If for some reason using the different colour marker does not work out, you can always use the backing for a rug of stripes or squares. The backing will never go to waste. This is a very forgiving way to draw because you get so many chances to make it right, or at least better.

You do not have to be a great drawer to design great rugs because design is really more about putting the elements together. Yet it is still important to learn a little bit about drawing if you want to design your own rugs, because you will gain confidence each time you approach the backing with your Sharpie. A basic foundation in drawing and most of all practice will give you all the skills you need for drawing for your hooked mats.

Drawing for rug hooking is different from drawing to create images in pen and ink, because when you draw for rug hooking you are really drawing a pattern to guide yourself. I always remind myself that though my drawing might not be perfect I can always adapt it when I hook. I approach my backing with my hook as if I were drawing or painting, not just filling in an area, especially when hooking those first lines when I begin a new rug.

Four Bowls.

Drawing was important to me as a child, but the truth is for years before I began hooking rugs I didn't really draw anything besides leaves or vines on the occasional poster that I would make for community projects. It was rug hooking that reminded me of the value of drawing again. Once I learned how to hook rugs I was quickly convinced that I needed to create my own drawings on my own backings.

When I draw for my mats I try to sketch out the basic idea as an outline. I don't really worry about putting in the interior details as I know I can do this with wool. I like to create loose sketches that show the basic shapes of things. They would almost be like colouring book drawings in that they just show the shape or the outline of the thing, except that the lines are much more rugged and sketchy.

Be thankful if you can't draw a straight line. You'll only do that for geometrics, and for that you can use a ruler. Hold your pencil loosely. We tend to grab writing instruments as though they are trying to escape our hands. Act as if it wants to be there, cuddle it. Draw a squiggly line with it. Let it perform a little dance in your hand without expecting any results.

Your drawings will look different from others' not only because you may have more or less skill but because you see things differently. Accept that you have your own view, your own way of seeing, and be grateful for that. Do not try to make your drawings look like someone else's, rather just draw like yourself, however that may be. Over the years I have learned that I tend to draw in a stylized way that is somewhat representative but not necessarily realistic. As I watch other artists I see that they too do the same thing and the basic drawings that they make are part of their style. Perhaps the drawings are not perfectly realistic but they certainly make you feel what it is the artist is trying to impart, and this to me is very important.

Design is about putting elements together more than it is about drawing, so remember that even the most inexperienced drawer can design rugs. It can be as simple as tracing circles and laying them out in a manner that is appealing and attractive to the eye. Still, the better you draw, the easier you will find design.

The Sketchbook

It is the essential tool. When I first started hooking rugs I drew in a Hilroy lined notebook. I had no idea about art, but I had an empty exercise book on hand, so that is what I used. When I was a little kid and needed paper I would scout through my father's books. He was an avid reader and I would scroll through his piles of paperbacks and rip out the pages in the front or the back that were blank and draw on those. After that, an unused Hilroy notebook looked really good to me. Now, of course, I always buy myself nice sketchbooks to make up for the paper shortage of my youth. I like two kinds of books: hardbound sketchbooks that open flat and coil-bound books.

My sketchbooks are like pools of ideas. I use them for writing, drawing, and pasting things into. Sometimes I just stick things in them, and they fall out years later when I'm pouring through my sketchbooks for old ideas. Finding these bits and pieces is like travelling through time. They remind me of all kinds of things that I would otherwise forget. A sketchbook is like an art journal of your life. Often I cannot draw everything the way it is because drawing is not my strong point, but I do find that if I make a rough sketch and write a few notes around it then I'm reminded of what I am seeing. You will never have time to make rugs of everything you put in your sketchbook. It is more of an art habit that makes you generally better at what you do. You get to be better at drawing, better at design, and as a result, better at hooking rugs.

My sketchbooks reflect every period of my life over the past twenty-two years. My first one was a lined Hilroy notebook.

It is important once you have had a sketchbook practice for a few years to review your books. By writing down or sketching your ideas, you capture them. The ideas you do not capture are lost forever, but those that you do capture are good forever, and you can always go back over them and sort through to pick out the ones you want to use to make rugs.

Without a sketchbook you will continue to draw a cat the way you did when you last drew one in grade six and you will lose all those ideas that pass through. A sketchbook is the place to collect your thoughts. Think of it as a repository for ideas, and then later it becomes kind of an idea mine. Set up a practice with your sketchbook. Keep a couple in different places so that you always have somewhere to put your thoughts and drawings.

Drawing Activities

DRAWING WARM-UPS

Here are some exercises to take the pressure off being perfect, to help you loosen up and draw more freely. If you practice them regularly you will get used to the pencil in your hand and feel more comfortable as you draw.

Cut a piece of paper into smaller pieces and on each piece write down an item to draw. Then fold each piece over, place them all in a jar and pull one out each time you want to do a warmup session. I would recommend words such as: house, carrot, woman, man, asparagus, bowl of flowers, egg, chicken, basket, box, onion, mushroom, car, lemon, apple, child, garden, rocks, cat, dog, book, sunglasses, nest, fish, bird, tree, etc.

First, try making five-second sketches, timing yourself. Or try drawing with the wrong hand: if you are left-handed draw with the right hand and vice versa. Or close your eyes and sketch the item.

STILL LIFE

Set yourself up a simple still life, perhaps some fruit and a bowl or a few flowers. Now follow the instructions for the drawing warm-ups, but give yourself ten minutes. Play with the still life until it is appealing to you.

After you have warmed up, allow yourself to sketch the still life for five minutes. Take a break for a few moments and walk around, then come back and allow yourself to sketch it for ten minutes. Take a break for a few moments, get a cup of tea, or stretch, then come back and draw the same thing again for fifteen minutes.

You can do this once a week, creating your own private drawing class, or you can invite another friend to join you. Change the still lifes each week. Do not worry about how good the drawing is: remember it is nothing more than practice and you will improve one sheet of paper at a time.

Drawing for rug hooking is the foundation for your design, but at the same time it is only just a sketch; you can change the lines as you hook.

EXPRESSIVE DRAWING

Take a sheet of paper in your sketchbook and divide it into eight rectangles. At the top of each rectangle write an expressive word such as: love, anger, joy, balance, loss, humility, fear, wonder.

Read each word and doodle what you feel. Drawing is not always about making things representational; it is also important to try to convey feeling or emotion in your sketches.

Drawing for Rug Design

Drawing for rug design can be easier than trying to draw realistically, but you do need to practice to get better at it. I believe that drawing for design is about finding simplified versions of whatever it is you want to hook and getting those lines down on the backing.

THUMBNAILS

Thumbnails are small sketches that set up your design in different ways. You simply draw the same idea over and over again in small boxes or rectangles on a piece of paper. Each time you draw it you change a little something or the shape of the box itself. Each little sketch works through a design idea for the rug. Creating thumbnails is a good way of working out a design idea without investing too much time in creating the actual rug.

When I was creating my poppies pattern book that we published in the studio, I made many thumbnail sketches and many extra poppy-themed rugs that never made it into the designs for the book. This is the benefit of working small. First the thumbnail sketches give you designs to choose from. You can quickly see how the flower looks to the left, to the right, or off-centre. After you choose the designs you like you can decide which are worth hooking. When you hook them small you get to see them take shape fairly quickly.

Style-builder Activity: THUMBNAIL SKETCHES IN WOOL OR INK

INK OR PENCIL

Take a section of your sketchbook and draw a bunch of thumbnails or quick sketches of design ideas. Do not worry if they are not exactly as you would like because they are just sketches, just carry on creating new sets of thumbnails. These sketches should be fast and easy to make. Do not labour over them; instead give yourself a whole bunch of choices. You can eliminate some later.

WOOL

Leave the ink drawings for a few days and come back to them. Take out a piece of backing, burlap or linen, and draw three quick sketches, not very big, something manageable that you can hook over the next few weeks. Leave these three pieces on the same piece of backing and work on them simultaneously. Move freely from one to the other. The designs can be related, or they can be completely different than each other. Accept that right now these rugs are not important, but are a learning tool. These rugs are sketches in wool. Do not focus on one piece, but instead keep skipping back and forth between them, making all three at once.

Repeat this activity every once in a while. You might come up with some interesting designs. If you do not want to make rugs of these sketches, then start again and create more designs using this same process. If you find you work out a really good thumbnail, you might decide to create a bigger rug inspired by one of them.

Susan Black and Joy Laking are local artists who suggested using these thumbnail boxes to sketch your idea. They are a great tool for trying the same design in different ways.

Making Marks: DRAWING WITH HOOK

Give a child a crayon and they will want to make a mark, on the wall if necessary. The oldest drawings we know of were carved in stone. Making marks is instinctual for us. We even have the expression "Make your mark," which means to make something your own.

So much about being inventive in rug hooking is about learning how to make your mark. Making your rugs look like your own rather than anyone else's is a real challenge. One of the ways a painter creates her own style is through brush strokes, and when I realized this I decided I could do the same with my hook.

Back when I started rug hooking I used a method of outlining and filling in that we still teach to the students who come to the studio each day to learn to hook rugs. This is a good way to begin your hooking. Over time, though, how you fill in those outlines is about how you make your mark, the direction and style of your hooking.

Because I am a bit compulsive when I hook rugs, the filling-in part became a little path of discovery. I found that once I had an area outlined I was free to hook in whatever direction I liked. This meant I just sort of followed my hook around, but over time I noticed I was kind of creating a style of marks or strokes on my rug.

Sometimes a mark is just the shape of an area that you hook again and again. A mark can be repeated and will often create a patterned effect in an area of the rug. Often I combine several different marks when I am hooking a big background area. Sometimes these form curves or swirls, other times circles or amoebas. When it comes to the design of larger pieces, I have learned that every area of the rug is a space to be filled in. Whether it's a portrait, a landscape, or a geometric, every time you make a line on a design you create a new space to fill in. I like to fill these in with loops hooked in interesting shapes. I consider the size, shape, colour, direction, and sometimes even the symbolic nature of a mark.

For example in a landscape rug, I often hook my marks so that they look and feel like the lay of the land. In the background of a rug with a central image or medallion, I will make any kind of fanciful mark I feel like and in a geometric rug, I usually follow the lines of the geometry.

My niece, Haley Perry, who studied fine art, wrote a series called Everyday Drawing for my blog in which she explains, "Mark-making is not as easy as you'd imagine. Mark-making should be varied and beautiful, with all the complexities of a well-thought-out poem." It is important to create a visual language for yourself that is expressive and beautiful and we can do this by learning to hook "strokes" that make our rugs more interesting. If you look at what you draw on a piece of paper as you stand by the phone you might get some idea what your natural "marks" are. What we do with a pen we can do with a hook just as easily. It's a matter of translating the idea from ink into wool. There are endless ideas for making marks. One great source of ideas is in painter's brush strokes.

As I have become more fanciful and playful in my designs I have found that I also like to create clear marks such as diamonds, circles, ovals, paisleys, squares, and teardrops in large areas of my designs occupied by skies, seas, hills, or backgrounds. It is so much fun to look at the rug as a series of areas that need to be filled in and then to choose a shape such as a paisley or a circle to fill the sky. This builds on a tradition in rug hooking, of working in simple shapes and colours, and giving it a more modern rendition. This idea can make a rug look very whimsical or playful, or it can appear more gentle or serious depending on the colours used and the design as a whole. I started working like this about five years ago after seeing a cocktail napkin that was created in a similar manner. The image on the napkin did not appeal to me at all but I saw a lot of merit in the idea. Design is everywhere. You just have to be paying attention.

Activity: MAKING MARKS ON THE PAGE

Take a sheet of paper and a pencil and doodle for ten minutes, filling the whole sheet of paper with your doodles.

Have a look at them. Are there some that are familiar and feel as if they might be *your* marks? Often people feel self-conscious when they set out to make marks like this. If that is the case for you, set a pad of paper by the phone or in front of the TV and work at it mindlessly. Your doodling will lead you to some good ideas for the kinds of lines and areas that you can hook in your rugs, and these will become your marks.

I could never spend enough time drawing. It is my biggest weakness in my art. If I could draw better I could do so much more.

Activity: MAKING MARKS WITH YOUR HOOK

Take five or six shades of a single colour and use them to hook freestyle in a 10-by-12-inch area. Move the wool in every way that you can possibly think of, creating marks of your own. Think of it as a tiny abstract, like the ones you would colour as a child, or as a doodle of rug hooking. You can always use the end result as a table mat or pillow top.

Transferring Patterns for Design

Years ago, before the Internet, before big hair and the 1980s, before Elvis, and before television, all over North America women were transferring rug-hooking patterns. Women coveted their pattern designs, saving them on heavy brown butcher paper so that they could be reused again and again. Women would copy the designs off wallpaper, fabric, from books, or fancy carpets. They were passed down from generation to generation and one set of patterns would make many mats. I have seen these wrinkled brown templates over the years, pulled out of trunks and suitcases and shown with pride. They were the creative tools of another generation and saved with respect.

There is a strong tradition of tracing or copying designs in rug hooking, but before you transfer a pattern make sure you have either designed it yourself, have permission, or that the design is copyright-free. Many artists make their living from their designs and it is important to respect their artistic property rights and pay for a design if you use it. If you like to create your own designs or have access to a copyright-free design that you want to trace, it is easy to transfer designs. You may also use this method to transfer the design ideas in the appendix of this book for your personal use.

WHAT YOU WILL NEED

• Yardstick/ruler or T-square
• Red dot tracer or wedding tulle
• Sharpie marker
• Linen or burlap backing
• T-pins to hold the tulle in place.

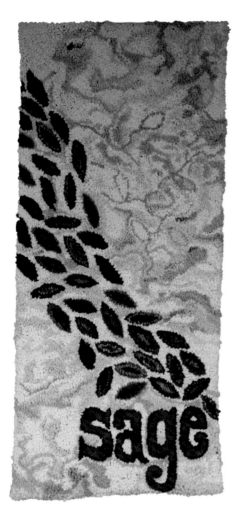

Sage, 24 by 54 inches. You can clearly see the marks made in this rug.

BASIC INSTRUCTIONS

You can transfer a pattern onto the backing of your choice using red dot tracer or wedding tulle, which is available at craft supply stores. (At the studio we often use wedding tulle instead of red dot tracer. Wedding tulle is used in exactly the same way and is more widely available at fabric stores.) You simply lay the tracing fabric over the pattern and trace it with a black permanent marker.

Use your ruler to create a straight edge around the outside of the pattern. You can then lay the tracer on your preferred backing and trace it again with the marker. The marker will seep t hrough onto your new backing.

When you are finished tracing, you can touch-up your design by retracing the pattern on the new backing. Now you are ready to start hooking.

CHAPTER FOUR

FROM SMALL TO BIG TO THEMES

Working Small

W*e live in a society that is focused on bigger and better and more, but many of* us know there is something about small that is powerful. Each one of us is small in the context of the world, one person among many, yet each of us matter. The power of small should never be dismissed. I love the feeling of starting a small rug and knowing it can be done within a day or two. It is empowering.

I find that I go back and forth from working big to working small. After working big for a while, working small feels like a relief. After working small for a while, working big seems like a retreat. The process for each is completely different. When I first started rug hooking I saw the big rugs as more important, but over time I have seen that I can learn just as much from a small rug, and that they can be just as, if not more, beautiful.

 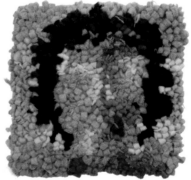 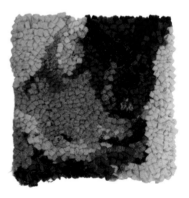

Three small rugs, about 6 by 6 inches each.

Rugs do not have to be big to matter. Small rugs can have a big impact either on their own or as part of a series of smaller works. Over the years I have created many bodies of work made up of small rugs. For the purposes of this book I would say a small rug is anything smaller than 12 inches by 12 inches (144 square inches altogether). With the wider widths of cloth I use and the thickness of the materials I am drawn to, I cannot really create much in the way of miniatures. Anything smaller than a pillow top I would consider a small rug. For my purposes I never make anything much smaller than a 2-by-3-inch ornament, and these I see more as decorations than rugs.

When you start a small rug you must consider it to be as valuable as any bigger piece you have done. If you take the attitude that it is just a small piece so it does not matter, then you are off to a bad start because you are not invested in it. I start a small rug with the same intention as I do when I start a big rug: I must make it as beautiful as I can. Intention is important. Often I see people start small pieces as something to whip up. I have done it myself. The truth is, if that is your approach you are more likely to make do with what is at hand rather than search for just the right fabric. Searching for just the right colour or fabric is very important in a small rug. There are fewer fabrics used, so each one matters more.

Over the years I have worked on a few themes in small rugs. I did a series of portraits of women called "Big Boned Girls" that were each about 5 by 12 inches. I've also done many houses and small landscapes. For small rugs I still work mainly with a number 6 or number 8 cut, but I will sometimes cut the number 8 in half to work out small details.

When I first began rug hooking I made many small pieces because they were affordable for customers when I would take my work to craft sales. I even hooked little pieces to attach to barrettes and packaged them as "Hair Rugs" and sold them at the Art Gallery of Nova Scotia gift shop. I find this funny now, but I really appreciated the cheques those little barrettes brought in when I was getting started. When I hooked really small pieces like this there was no to create a design, so they were mainly about colour. I find the same goes for small ornaments. There are only a few simple designs that seem to work well for creating tiny 2-by-3-inch designs. The principles of keeping things simple are never more important than when you are hooking small pieces.

Finding a theme to work on is a great way to create small rugs. I have found that when I do this I will create many rugs that are similar yet distinct, and that can hang beautifully on their own or together. I find that when I work on themes such as small landscapes, if I make them all the same size I can choose to hang them as a diptych or triptych. Hanging small pieces together gives a bigger visual impact in a room. Sometimes you have a spot that needs a bigger piece of art and though you might not be ready to make a very large rug you might be willing to make several small pieces to hang together.

Because of the design of my Cheticamp frame, when I am working small there are times when I focus on several pieces at once. My frame allows me to work an area of 18 by 40 inches, so I will often draw several smaller rugs onto one piece of backing. If they are related thematically I will work on all of them at once, going

Moon Scene, 4 by 6 inches. Small rugs somehow seem more interesting once they are framed.

from one rug to another. If they are individual rugs unrelated to each other in theme, I will work on one and finish it before starting another. Once all the hooking is done I will take them off the frame and bind them individually.

I have learned that there are many designs that do not translate well into small rugs. An image that has a lot of detail will not work as a tiny rug. You need room to show detail. Unless you want to work in a very fine cut it is essential that you omit some of the detail of the design and pare it down to a simply lined drawing that can be expressed with thicker cuts of wool. Simplifying the lines of your design is important when working small. I also find that big contrasts in colour can be helpful in defining and distinguishing areas of small rugs, since you won't have room for lots and lots of outlining. When you outline fine details in a small rug they often get muddled and appear big and unshapely.

Tiny decorative owls, 3 by 2 inches, on a branch. Sometimes I want to make things that are purely decorative. Not everything has to be art. (See appendix for owl template.)

Activity: HOOKING ORNAMENTS

I have made many small rugs over the years, mostly for small wall hangings or table mats, but I have also made tiny ornaments to hang on a tree or decorate a parcel. These ornaments are playful little designs that I use as small gifts. When I make small hooked ornaments I do not bind them in the traditional way. Instead I finish the hooking, turn them over to the back side and spread white carpenter's glue (I use Lepages) all over the hooked area. Let it dry overnight and the next day you will find that it has hardened and almost plasticized. You can then cut the ornaments out and sew a ribbon to each one for hanging. I have also glued magnets to them and used them on the fridge. This is a great project to get children started rug hooking.

TIPS FOR WORKING SMALL

• Keep your design simple. Do not have too many details or they will get muddied when you hook.

• For small rugs that will never be used on the floor and are mainly decorative, I often use primitive burlap because it is inexpensive. Scottish burlap, which is a more even grid, is great for geometrics. I use linen for larger pieces or anything going on the floor because it is stronger.

• Treat the small rug as important when choosing wools and colours. Remember, you want to make it as beautiful as you can.

• Do not overdo it on textured yarns and wools in a small piece because they can overwhelm the rug and can make it hard to distinguish the design.

• In small pieces you can still use lots of colours.

• Be deliberate in your choice of the widths of fabric you use. I mix widths and use narrower cuts in smaller rugs.

• When you work small it is still important to hook directionally and consider the marks you make as this can enhance the rug.

• Smaller pieces make great series. I will often choose a theme and work on it, creating a body of smaller pieces.

• Save all your leftover strips from bigger projects in a bin and use these for your small projects.

• The great thing about working small is that if it is not working you can rip it out and change it up without losing a lot of time.

Chasing Klimt, 53 by 71 inches.

Working Big

After I have been working on a series of small rugs for a time, I always feel like I want to work on a bigger rug. The same goes after finishing a big piece: I want to go back to smaller pieces. This has been my pattern of hooking for years. I love both of them at different times. I think of a big rug as anything 5 feet by 3 feet (15 square feet) or larger. Of course, what a person considers big is really dependent on experience. For some it might be 4 by 3 feet.

Creating a big rug is a bit of an oxymoron because it is equally about planning and letting go. You need to plan out the basics—the wool you'll need, the frame you'll use and of course your design—but if you plan too much, you risk becoming bored before you get halfway through it. It is important that as you hook a large rug you allow yourself to be spontaneous and creative. I never colour-plan the entire rug because I want the hooking to be a process and I know that when I add one colour, it will define the next colour. In large rugs, I am also open to changing elements of the design as I work through it. A large rug is very process-oriented because it takes so long to hook. Working through it is a slow task of showing up at the frame day after day, often for several months. It takes a great deal of commitment and you need to know that you love the process and that you want to hook. So though you need to plan, it is also important that you work organically. Let things change and develop as you go.

As I write these words I am nearing the end of a very large rug that I began nearly two months ago. Though I only have an hour or so left to hook on it, I really have no idea if the rug is anything like what I set out to make. I am hooking it because I love the process, the motion of pulling up the wool loop by loop, and because of that I am willing to risk all this time and wool on the possibility that it will be beautiful. I set out to make a modern-looking design from a simple pattern of circles inside of squares. My rug is rolled on my Cheticamp frame so I can only see a panel at a time. What I imagine in my head as the completed rug will be very different than the actual completed rug. I know this from experience, yet all throughout I continued to work with the picture in my head as the guide. As much as it is a risk to have spent nearly two months creating something and not really being sure of its beauty, it is also very exciting. There is an element of surprise to hooking big rugs because you never know what it will look like until it is on the floor.

When I first started hooking I made mostly mid-sized pieces of 20 by 30 inches or so, and after creating many small and mid-sized rugs for craft sales I decided that it would be a good challenge to create a room-sized rug. I wanted to see what a really large hooked rug would look like on the floor of my home. The first thing I needed to consider was what kind of frame I could hook it on. For me keeping my wool taut on my frame matters a lot, so I had a Cheticamp

My Cheticamp frame is essential for working big.

frame made with 6-foot arms. This allowed me to hook a rug 6 feet wide by any length. Your choice of frame is important if you decide to hook a large rug. You must be comfortable and want to get at the rug, as it will take many, many hours to complete. You can use a quilting frame or a laptop frame. The problem with a laptop frame is that as you get a portion of the rug done it will become very heavy to hold in your hand as you hook.

You also need to have a defined colour palette and plenty of wool on hand. Defining a colour palette for your rug is different from colour planning. You want to be able to choose the colours as you go along, keeping the creation of the rug organic and the process more interesting. Creating a very large rug is like a relationship: you do not want to feel as if everything is mapped out for you. Leave room for a few surprises along the way. Rather than colour planning, create a set of colours— six or eight shades and textures that work well together—that define the tone and feeling of your rug. You can add many more shades within these main colours as you go. You can even throw in another few colours as long as they work well with the original six or eight.

Large rugs require many more colours than most small or mid-sized rugs because there is so much more space to fill. Whatever area you are hooking, in a larger piece you will often need to blend and mix several colours together. For example if your large rug had a green leaf in it, one shade of green will not do unless you want a very flat, primitive look. You will have to mix your shades to keep it interesting and add depth to the rug.

As important as it is to think about the space you are creating the rug for, I have to be honest here: over the years I have made about eight room-sized rugs. I set out on most of them with the intention of making them for a certain area in my home, selecting size and colour based on the space. Each time I got so involved in the rug that I let go of my original intentions and let the rug grow on its own. In the end none of them ever really got used in the space they were intended for. Personally I find that I get invested in the rug itself and I am willing to forget about the space I intended it for, but here are a few things to keep in mind: Large rugs need room to be viewed if you plan to hang them on the wall. You do not want to squeeze them into a space. Make sure that you have some space around the perimeter of the rug on the wall. It is also important that you have room to step back from the rug so you can see it.

Many large rugs are made for the floor, as carpets. If you are planning to make a carpet, I think design is very important. You will need to consider that you will be looking down at the rug instead of viewing it on a wall. I find that a carpet that is designed for the floor can often hang well on a wall, but that a rug designed for the wall does not always look great on a floor. When I hook carpets I like to create a design that can be viewed well and easily when you look down upon it, and one that looks good from all angles you might approach it from. In creating the designs, I often choose all-over patterns or modify the design with a border or a repeated pattern that you can see from all sides. I really do not like a pictorial image on the floor. It just looks odd to me.

Think seriously about what backing you might like to use. Scottish burlap comes in very wide widths, as does monk's cloth. Personally I prefer sewing together two pieces of linen as this allows you to create very wide patterns. You will have to hook through two layers of linen where they overlap, but this is not difficult. Most linen is 5 or 6 feet wide, so this method will allow you to make carpets 10 to 12 feet wide by any length.

You cannot wash hooked mats, so if your carpet is in a high-traffic area, cleaning it may become an issue. The old-fashioned technique of turning your rug upside down in freshly fallen snow still works beautifully; it allows the dust to fall out. I will also spot wash or sponge an area of the rug with warm water and some gentle soap if I need to, making sure the water stays on the surface of the rug. Never ever throw a rug in the washing machine or immerse it fully in water. This is hard on the backing and will wear out the rug.

TIPS FOR WORKING LARGE

- Make sure you have lots of wool, enough to complete the rug. I like to save some of each colourway, setting it aside in case I need it further along in the rug.

- You do not have to use every colour throughout the entire rug. You can balance colour by using similar shades in different areas.

- If you are making a rug for the floor, consider using linen as your backing as it is very durable.

- Have the rug set up on a frame in a visible place so you will be inclined to do a little work on it every day. It is important to create a habit of working on the rug daily so you will see progress.

- If you find you are getting tired of the rug as you work your way through it, do not put it away. Instead make a design or colour change, adding new yarns and wools to the palette you have decided upon to keep you interested. (This is why I do not like to colour plan the whole thing.)

- Do not get stalled by not knowing what colour to put in a certain area. Choose a colour and hook it. Remember, it is easy once the rug is hooked to remove a small area and re-hook it in a different colour. Rug hooking is a very forgiving craft: you do not have to unravel a big area to get at your mistake, you can just remove the little area you want to change.

- Borders are a great way to tie a large floor rug together because it unifies the whole piece.

- Large rugs require a huge push to the finish, so it is important to keep your focus on finishing the rug rather than on making everything perfect.

- Embrace the surprise. You will not really know what the rug is going to look like until the whole thing is completed. Be patient with it.

- When you design a rug, one option is to design a quarter of the rug and repeat the design four times to create a pattern.

- You can also create a smaller pattern and repeat it many times for an all-over patterned effect.

Sometimes when I am working on a theme it feels like I could go on forever. Then one day, suddenly, I am done and on to the next thing. Owls, approx. 8 by 18 inches each.

Working on a Theme

I cannot help but work on a theme. I have made so many rugs over the years, but there are themes that I come back to again and again: fish, people, big-boned girls, trees, landscapes, seascapes, villages, flowers, and houses. You can create a theme out of any word or idea, which offers endless possibilities. This way of working also helps you develop style because it makes you focus on your own way of doing things. It gives you the opportunity to develop a unified body of work and you will begin to see your style emerge. It is a chance to explore your natural way of doing things.

Working on a theme is often suggested for small rugs because it is a great way to work through a series of ideas without taking up too much time or energy but when you work on a theme, it is the theme not the size that matters. You could work them all small, all large, or you can mix it up. It is completely up to you.

Generally I will focus closely on a theme for a period of few years, creating many rugs on a similar idea, but I will also move in and out of a theme over many years. For example I do not think I will ever leave the textured landscape theme behind as I am drawn back to it again and again, loving the freedom of using so many interesting materials. But for about three years I made small portraits working on the theme of big-boned girls and for now I have left that theme, feeling no real desire to continue to hook these even though I still have hundreds of ideas for them. I do not feel that I have abandoned small portraits altogether. I'm just not sure right now. I like to let the artist in me (and time) determine this. I am open to whatever inspiration comes, but I have found that I cannot successfully force myself to work on a theme simply because there is a demand for such work.

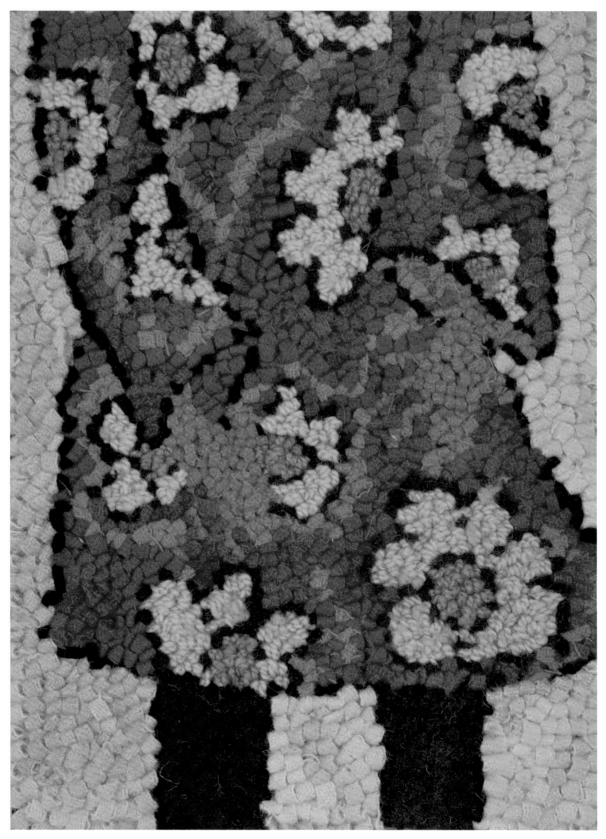

New Dress, 8 by 14 inches.

When you work on a theme, you might find you'll make five or six rugs or fifty or sixty over a period of years. There is no set standard. You might need breaks, working on one theme for a while, then breaking into something else for a period of time. You can set out with an idea of how many rugs of a particular theme you might want to make and what size they might be, but be open to change. Don't force yourself to plug away through a theme uninspired. It is important to love and be excited by what you are making.

A theme works best when there is focus and consistency. Think a lot about what theme you want to hook and narrow it down to a few simple elements if you can. For example, if I chose the theme of the ocean, I might focus on a couple of elements, such as a starfish or seaweed, as the basis for the theme rather than trying to fit in too many elements. If your theme is too broad it might be difficult to know what to hook. It is important to keep your focus, while at the same time facing the challenge of being open to change. You can also create themes around a colour palette, creating a series of rugs based on a similar group of colours. Artists have done this for years, having their blue period or white period. Choosing a colour pallette as a theme does not mean focusing only on one colour either; it could be a group of colours that create a certain mood.

You want the themed rugs that you create to be tied in together in some way, or perhaps a variety of ways. Sometimes when I work on a theme I create diptychs or triptychs that hang together. These pieces I often hook on the same frame, with a space left between them for binding. Often I will unite these rugs by hooking similar shades in each piece, or by using the line of the basic design and allowing it to flow from one rug into the next so that the design travels throughout.

Style-builder Activity: WORKING ON A THEME

This activity is about making a series of rugs, so expect to spend weeks or months on it as you go about your creative process. Choose an idea or a theme for yourself based on something you love and explore it completely in a series of small rugs. If you choose a starfish, say, go get some starfish, read about starfish, gather images of starfish…then put all of this away. Go to your frame with your backing and play with designing a series of three to five small pieces. You can look at things up close, from far away, in multiples, in context. You choose the idea and the design format you want to explore it in. Working on a theme is a great exercise in developing style because you begin to understand how you see things. We all have our own perspective, our own way of seeing, and as we continue to create, this way of seeing emerges and we can call that our style.

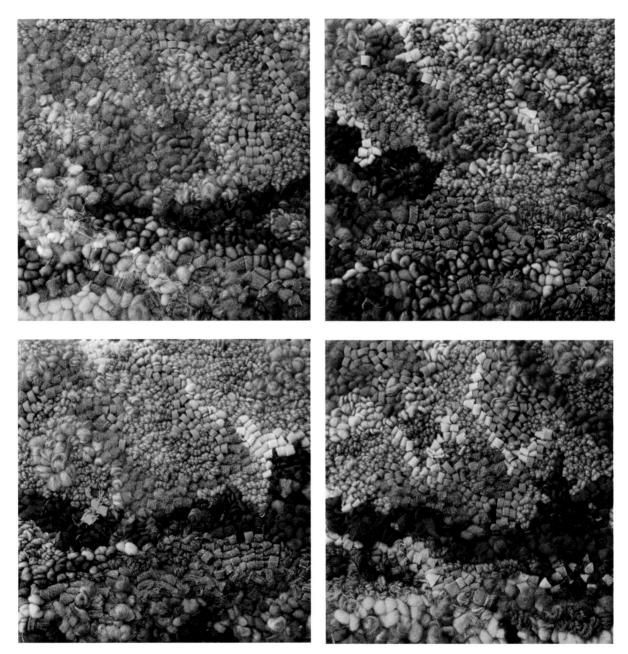

Field Work, four 4-by-10-inch squares.

CHAPTER FIVE

THE MAGIC OF MATERIALS

Hooking with Wool Fabric

W*hen I first started hooking I used only wool cloth. I was a bit of a purist about it.* In 1990 there were lots of recycled wools available. I would go to second-hand stores and gather old wool jackets and coats, blankets, skirts, and shirts. I would take them home, wash them and dry them, rip them apart at the seams, roll each piece of fabric, and tie it with an elastic band to store.

I hated to use new wool off the bolt because I loved the recycling aspect of rug hooking. At that time I was more of a traditionalist in that I wanted to make rugs the way my grandmother would have, using old clothes and hooking on burlap bags.

In the twenty-two years since, rug hooking has once again gained an incredible popularity and there are now women hooking rugs in many communities around North America. It has had a grassroots revival because it is so easy to teach rug hooking and to learn it. There is only one stitch, and the rest is all about what you can do with colour and design.

The other thing that has made rug hooking grow is the community built around it. In small communities and big cities, people gather in community halls, homes, and church basements for their weekly hook-ins. They get together regularly to chat, plan their rugs, and hook them. These growing communities are often very open to teaching new people the basics, and so the craft has grown from one person teaching another.

This new popularity has meant that recycled wool has become harder and harder to find. As well fewer and fewer people are wearing woolen clothing these days, so there is no new influx of woolen cloth into the second-hand market. Much of what we find now are blends or acrylics that look and feel a lot like wool, but wool itself is a special fabric because there are so many textures

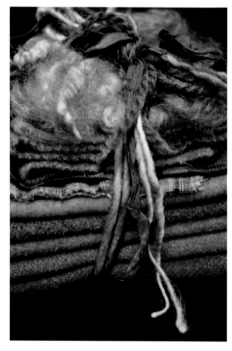

Putting wool together in bundles inspires me to hook.

Recycled wool is getting harder to find as people wear wool clothing less and less.

available. Its natural softness means that its structure is pliable and will blend with other wools. It is also extremely durable.

Whenever you go to thrift or second-hand stores, be on the lookout for wool garments to use in your rug hooking. Be open to all different weights of wool. As you try the different types, you will decide which you like best. I particularly like wool flannel, but have learned that if I only use this weight of wool in my rugs it makes the finished results less interesting. So I also keep my eye out for angora sweaters, as they come in such pretty colours, and any other finely knit sweaters in cashmere, silk, or wool blends. You can cut sweaters across the body and up and down the arms. I often try cutting the strips in different directions because the knit and cut of the fabric will be different when it is hooked. Sweaters tend to roll in on themselves or curl outwards as they are hooked. Women's skirts are always great because they come apart so easily. All you have to do is remove the waistband and you have a nice large piece of wool. I try to avoid very thinly weighted wool serge as I do not like the feel of hooking with it, but I will a little if I cut the pieces wide to add texture to a rug.

Blankets are another thing I am always on the lookout for because there is so much cloth in them. They often come in creams and whites, which is great for dyeing, and they are so soft to hook with. Around the Amherst area many people have little cottages that have been in their families for generations, and there are often old wool blankets in these cottages that have not been used for years. Every once in a while I am gifted with one of these. Blankets hook up nice and high, and they have lots of body. One of my favourite wools to work with is wool jersey, but it is hard to find. I love the way it curls when you hand-cut it and the stretchiness of the fabric as you hook it.

Mohair shawls and blankets and boiled wool jackets are great for adding interesting texture to your mats, but be careful not to wash these in hot water or throw them into the dryer because they shrink up and felt on you. Handwash these in warm water and dry on the line, then hand-cut them in nice wide strips; they will pull apart easily.

Wash all second-hand wools as soon as you bring them in the house. This is really important simply for the value of working with clean wool but also because rugs once they are hooked are not washable. I store my washed wool folded on open shelves because I want to be able to see it and choose my colours. Second-hand wool is a great source of cloth for hooking. Whenever you travel stop in to second-hand stores such as the Salvation Army. Maybe you will get lucky and find a shop that the local rug hookers have missed.

The other source of cloth is new wool off the bolt. This is a more expensive alternative but you can always buy 1/4- or 1/2-yard pieces. In fact, for the purposes of building a good stash, you are better off with four 1/4-yard shades of similar greens than you are with a 1-yard piece of a single green. However, if it is a great green that you know you will love, take the opportunity to build your stash and get a yard. Wool in lighter shades is perfect for dyeing and overdyeing. You can use new wool off the bolt without washing it, but many people prefer to wash and dry their wool first because it makes the wool slightly thicker, increasing the nap and making it softer to use. So much about hooking is enjoying the feeling of the wool as it slips through your fingers.

We dye new wool cloth for the studio so we have good colour ranges. These can be cut by a machine or by hand.

Once you gather your wool you will prepare it for rug hooking by tearing it apart and cutting it into strips. You can simply fold your wool and hand-cut it with a pair of short-shanked scissors. I do this all the time as I get into my hooking and do not want to leave the frame to cut my wool. Many rug hookers also use mechanical wool cutters. I use the Bolivar Wool Cutter, which is made a few hours away from me here in Nova Scotia. The mechanical cutters cut the wool on a number system, with 3 being the narrowest at 3/32 of an inch and 16 being the largest at 1/2 an inch. I

Whether I hook with yarn or wool cloth, I like to grab the edge of my material with my hook to pull it through.

prefer numbers 6 (3/16 inch) or 8 (1/4 inch). For wider cuts, I hand-cut my own. For narrower cuts used for tiny details, I will take a number 8 and cut it in half.

Hooking with wool cloth is very rewarding, especially when you can mix beautiful new and found materials. I prefer found materials but have learned that if I limit myself to them I limit what I can do with my art. When I first started rug hooking there was much more access to recycled materials, but that has changed with the times, and so I have had to as well.

Hooking with Yarn and Cloth

Often people believe that hooking with yarn is different than hooking with cloth but it is really the same thing. The method and technique is exactly the same with yarn as it is with cloth. There is just a little difference in the way you catch the yarn with your hook underneath the backing: you will want to catch the yarn as a whole so that you do not split the wool.

When I first started making kits to sell in stores, I decided to make them with yarn because cutting fabric into strips was so labour intensive. I hooked the entire design in yarn but I never felt right about it because that was not the way I hooked myself.

In the studio I like to be authentic. In fact I have a carving by Nova Scotia artist Heather Lawson, the word *truth* written in stone, hanging above my desk. I might fib a little about stuff like how long it takes to make a rug (I have no idea!), but I try to be as honest as I can and that stone is a good reminder for me of my father, who said, "Always tell the truth."

A rug hooked completely in one type of yarn looks very different from a rug using cloth cut into strips. For that reason, I have never really liked rugs hooked in all Briggs and Little, or all MacAusland's wool yarn. As you can imagine selling something you are not crazy about is no fun—and hard to sell! Eventually, I abandoned the idea of yarn kits and starting selling just cloth kits.

At that time, about fifteen years ago in the late nineties, I moved completely away from yarn. After the kit experience, and not really feeling good about it, I decided not to bother with the plainer yarns. Essentially I threw out the baby with the bathwater, which was not a good move because yarn itself has many good qualities. It took me about eight years to come back to an appreciation of wool yarns, both fancy and simple. At first I was attracted to the fancy yarns and the handspun ones and for several years I stuck close to that. What I was ignoring was the effect that a plain yarn has when it is used as a texture and set against cloth or a fancier yarn. It took me years to rediscover this.

I learned that it is important never to dismiss a material because each one offers its own presence to a rug, whether it is plain and simple or complex and interesting. You do not want only one or the other. I am open to hooking almost any yarn of any weight as long as I like the material. That said, I prefer wool or silk.

Hooking with yarn is really no more difficult than hooking with wool cloth. I hold my hook exactly the same way and treat the yarn as if it were a strip of cloth. The only difference is that the yarn is a different texture and it comes in balls or skeins. The technique is pretty much the same.

Adding yarn to my rugs has led to so many new possibilities for colour and texture. I am so glad I am not a purist about wool cloth.

HELPFUL TECHNIQUES FOR HOOKING WITH YARN

• Collect a selection of yarn, choosing a variety of materials and textures. Do not overlook the simpler, plainly spun yarns as they add a nice contrast to the texture of cloth and fancy yarns.

• When you purchase a skein you can wind it into a ball or you can unwind the skein and cut it on each end. The second method (left) will give you many long strips of yarn to hook with.

• When you cut a skein for strips you can tie the whole thing in a knot so that it does not get tangled up.

• Share your skeins with another rug hooker. In our studio we will cut a skein in half for you, but this may not be the case in other places. Instead, shop with a friend and split the skeins so you each have more variety of colour.

• When a yarn is fine you can hook up two or three, even five or six strips of it at a time. You will find that the amount of strips you hook at a time will vary the texture of your rug.

• When you buy a skein of yarn that is hand dyed in several colourways you can take half of it and have the strips in the colourways so that it is mottled. You can then take the other half and cut it into individual colours. This is good for using throughout a larger rug to create colour balance. It also optimizes the yarn, giving you several colour options for your hooking.

• Get to know what each different texture of yarn can do and where it works best.

• Pull a yarn a little higher or hook it a little tighter to shift the texture a bit.

• Yarn can be dyed just like cloth, so when you shop for it be sure to buy some in light and natural colours.

• When you dye yarn you will get different effects if you leave some twirled in skeins and some as long hanks.

Fleece and Other Materials

When I discovered that I could hook wool fleece before it had been spun I felt like I had a whole new material to work with. I loved it because the fleece worked up quite differently from cloth or yarn. It had a loose, sculptural quality to it when I hooked it high with lots of space between the loops, and it had a hard, lumpy quality when I hooked it lower and tighter. Both were useful in my mats depending on what I was hooking.

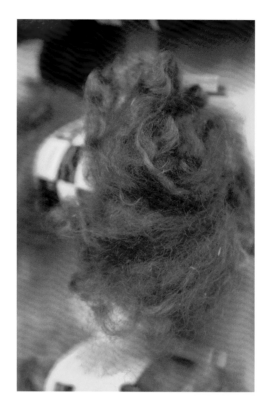

Fleece comes lots of different ways and varies depending on the animal or type of sheep it comes from. For example alpaca fleece is very different from goat fleece, which is very different from sheep fleece. When I am choosing fleece I am mostly looking for longer locks of hair and I particularly like fleece with lots of curl to it. Often I have been offered wool fresh off the sheep, but I am reluctant to take it because washing and preparing the fleece is a big job. I like to buy fleece from a farmer after they have washed it and got out all the bits of grass and dung. For me it is worth the extra money to purchase it washed and cleaned and ready to hook. When you buy it natural it is great for dyeing, but some farmers sell it washed and dyed at a premium price. Other times I buy it carded or combed, which smoothes the fleece out and makes it into a long continuous strip. Carded fleece has a different look to it when it is hooked than natural fleece does, as the natural curl of the fleece has been combed smooth once it has been carded.

Fleece and sari silks are great for small details.

All fleece can be hooked and it wears well. But you will find that how thick a strip of fleece or how much you hook will vary how the loops look. I like to take fairly narrow strips of wool fleece, less than a 1/4-inch thick, pull them gently to stretch out the length of the strip, and then hook it. I do not like to hook thick strips of fleece because I find it loses its interest and gets almost lumpy; the wool seems to clump together and does not have much movement. When I hook the thinner strips the wool looks sculpted and airy.

Silks and other fine materials make an impact in hooked rugs. Over the last few years I have used a lot of recycled sari silk from Nepal in rugs. This thick, coarse material looks like a shiny rag and adds interesting texture. You can also use recycled silk ties or shirts to get a similar effect.

Any quality material that you come across is worth exploring by trying to hook it in your mat. It is important to enjoy the process of using the material; keeping this in mind will help you decide which materials are right for you to hook with.

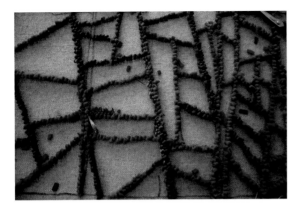

Outline in a fabric that contrasts either by colour or texture.

Sampler Activity: YARN SAMPLER PILLOW/RUG PROJECT

Exploring yarns has given me a lot of freedom to create interesting textures in my rugs. You might try creating a sampler of yarns for yourself. With this method you can create a variety of rugs or pillows.

- Create a very basic design of squares or circles and use one colour to outline the whole project. Choose a strong colour that will contrast with the yarns you are filling in.

- Now fill in each square with a different yarn.

If you want, for reference, you can draw the pattern on a piece of card stock and glue a strip of the yarn to the corresponding block that you hooked in the pattern. Most likely you will remember the yarn you used from looking at it hooked, but if you want a reference this is an easy way to make one for yourself.

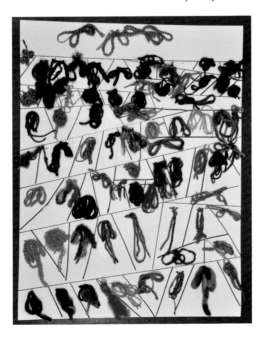

I created an abstract landscape for my sampler outlining the geometric-styled landscape in dark plum and going through my studio and looking at all my different yarns, filling in each oddly shaped area with a different yarn. I liked the results a lot. It has a modern look and a great reminder of what each yarn can do. I saved a sample of each so that I can identify them in the sampler, but I find when I look at the sampler hooked I can clearly identify each yarn. The hooked rug itself is a sampler and though it makes a beautiful rug or wall hanging, I think it also functions as a good learning tool. I have enclosed a similar pattern in the back of the book (see p. 138) that you can enlarge and use to create your own geometric-landscape sampler.

Abstract Landscape Yarn Sampler. I wanted to experiment with many different yarns in one rug.

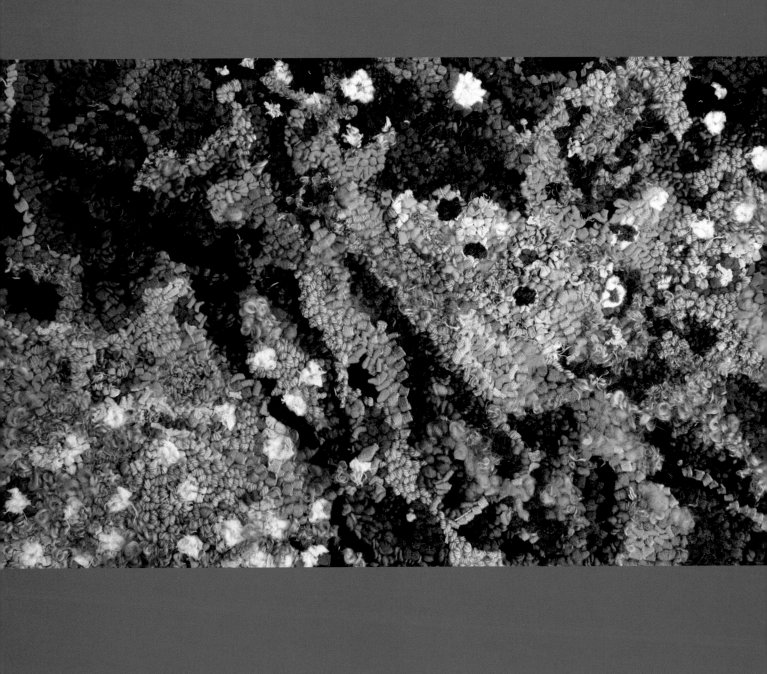

CHAPTER SIX

HOOKING WITH STYLE

Understanding Materials and Capturing Movement

The choice of materials to hook are endless. Practically any material that you can form into a strip can be hooked. I like to hook mainly wool and silk. I love these two materials because of the way they look and feel. They are both luxurious and strong and I believe that you get out of something what you put into it. If you hook with poor-quality fabrics, it affects the end result. Occasionally I will throw in a bit of velvet, a strip of cotton, or a polyester, but these are few and far between in my rugs.

Through My Life, Coral Abstract, 26 by 52 inches.

The important thing to remember is that every material will have its own voice or way of being in a hooked rug. No two materials will act alike. The real goal is to know what each material can do and how it will react in the rug. Knowing the effect of a material gives you a better ability to show what you want to with your hooking.

The material we are going to explore here is wool. It comes primarily from sheep, and in itself it has hundreds of variations. You cannot really begin to understand rug hooking until you begin to understand the nature of wool, what it can do, and the many forms it comes in. I have been hooking rugs for twenty years and I am still surprised by the nature of certain wools and what they look like when they are hooked up.

Wool is processed in hundreds of different ways and the result is that there are endless varieties of textures, cloths, fleeces, yarns, and fibres to hook with. The same goes for silk. Different sheep, different animals (alpacas, llamas), provide different types of wool. Once you get that wool, you can leave it natural, card it, spin it in a variety of different ways, or weave it in endless designs.

Wool itself as a material has infinite possibilities. At its best it is luxurious, soft, and natural. That is why I love it. I love how it responds in your hands. It responds to pressure, it is soothing to hold, to slip through your fingers. It is a material fit for kings and queens, for the richest among us. Yet it is available to everyone, right off the back of a lowly sheep from the field. What could be better than that? (Well, maybe homemade butter, but that's another thing altogether.) People who love

THINGS YOU NEED TO KNOW ABOUT MATERIALS

• You need a lot of different wools in lots of different colours and textures if you want to be creative in your rugs. It is not like painting where you can mix up a colour on the spot. You need a big selection in order to be able to have freedom in your choices as you're working.

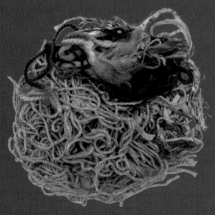

• If you have a yard of, say, blue, it is better to have three shades of blue to make that yard, than a yard of one shade. You need several shades in order to show movement and shading. This allows you to mix colours and create new colours by blending several together. It also allows you to show shadow and light.

wool—and there are many of us—understand that its natural and luxurious qualities make you commit to it as a material to work with because it is so responsive to colour, texture, and design. Wool is tactile, and if you are going to spend hours and hours holding a fabric you want to enjoy the process as much as the end result.

Beware of Moths

Moths are attracted to wool stored for long periods of time, especially in dark places. It is important to clean your studio, handling every piece of wool a few times a year. I like to take a day and go through every piece of wool in the studio, moving it around, shaking it out, and rearranging it by colour every once in a while. This not only gets me handling my stash, and knowing what I have to work with, but also lets me ensure my studio is clean and free of any moth problems.

Moths are an issue for anyone who collects wool. It is not the adult moths flying around that causes you the real problem, but their larvae. When a moth lays its eggs it attaches itself to wool and the larvae feed off the wool, boring a hole in it. I have found that the very best prevention for moths is pheromone traps. You can find them to order online if you just Google "moth control." The traps use pheromones to lure the moths into a sticky trap and prevent the eggs from ever being laid. I place the traps around my studio as a preventative measure and have had no problem with moths since I began using them. But even if I did not see a moth for years I would still use them just in case.

- You cannot store your wool in plastic bins in the basement if you want to hook beautiful rugs. You need to be able to see it and be inspired by it. The materials are beautiful in themselves. So get a shelf and fold your wool like you imagine Martha Stewart might fold her towels so you can see it, be inspired by it, and be tempted to use it.

- Do not skimp on your favourite wool, saving it up for something special. Use it before you forget you have it. Do not be like an old lady who dies with all her new underwear in the bottom drawer. Materials are abundant; they are meant to be used up so you can get inspired all over again by new ones.

- You need to collect materials and then wash and clean them as soon as you get them. I will use new wool straight off the bolt without washing, but sometimes I like to wash it just to fluff it up a bit.

- If you're using recycled wool, make sure you tear it apart into useable-sized pieces as it takes much less room to store wool that is torn apart, with linings and buttons removed, than it does full articles of clothing. It is also much easier to use once you are ready to cut it up. Even when I store blankets I like to cut them into pieces of about 20 by 12 inches so that I can grab a single piece to cut up rather than unfold a whole blanket.

You can learn so much just by experimenting with small squares or circles and many different fabrics.

Activity: EXPERIMENTING WITH A NEW FABRIC

Though I primarily hook with wool, I think it is important to be open to new materials and to experiment. I try not to hold fast to any rules because growing your art is not so much about rules, and it does not benefit from following rules that prevent you from exploring.

For this activity try using a new material, something from around the house, something you never hooked with before. Find some old discarded piece of cloth or clothing or other fibre, and hook it onto a backing as a sampler. You do not have to use it or make anything with it. Just try something odd. Remember, anything that can be cut into a strip can be hooked. Be adventurous and surprise yourself. Imagine what a piece of ribbon, string, rope, a strand of linen, or a strip of plastic might look like hooked. These unusual materials can sometimes lead to great new details in your rugs and I have learned that sometimes it is the tiniest detail that makes a rug really beautiful.

Mary's Pillow. Mary works in the studio with me on Tuesdays. She took one of my online courses and made this pillow.

Activity: SQUARE SAMPLER

If you want to hook beautiful rugs you have to get very familiar with materials and what they can do. This morning I pulled about twenty-five different types of materials out of my stash and hooked them. I then took a picture of the material next to a small hooked square. This was an exercise in getting familiar with what the wools hook up like. You could also create a sampler by gluing a piece of the wool beside the hooked square. I chose to take photographs because this allowed me to see more of the original rug.

As I hooked those squares, I thought about the idea of hooking for the sake of hooking. After the exercise I had a long narrow area on my frame covered in random squares of different sizes in no particular order. It occurred to me that what I was doing was creating a bit of a design challenge. I could just rip these off the frame and forget about them or I could seek a challenge with it. What kind of design could I create from these random squares that I had made purely as an exercise? I drew some lines around the edges of the squares and created a rug. This rug will be designed as it goes along; it will be an exercise in hooking for the sake of hooking and in responsiveness. I had saved some of the extra wool from the little squares together in a pile and once I was done with the squares I began to outline them with the leftovers from other squares. From there, we will have to see. So your challenge is to create a sampler or squares, really using the exercise to get to know a selection of different types of wool. From there I encourage you to then create a design based on the random squares that you hooked while carrying out this exercise. I am going to use this lesson on hooking the ocean to help demonstrate my ideas about both materials and movement.

Understanding Movement: HOOKING THE OCEAN

The sea is always moving; it never lets up. There is always motion. Even in the stillest and calmest of times, there is subtle movement on the water. I have hooked oceans many times and I have used hundreds of different types of wools to create them. Some oceans have used ten or eleven different wools, or even more. You can get as complicated as you like, but you can also create a simple ocean mix using four shades of blue.

SIMPLE OCEAN MIX

• a light-blue tweed

• a variegated blue yarn with some royal blue and other shades in it

• a mauve/blue tweed

• a solid blue similar in shade to the light-blue tweed

TIPS FOR HOOKING WATER

• Take some of each cloth and cut it up on number 8 cut tweed.

• Cut some of the blue and mauve tweed by hand, just so you can add a little textural effect. If the yarn is lightweight, I sometimes hook two strands at once.

• I like to draw a few waves or wavy lines in the area I am going to use for ocean. These lines will act as a guide for my hooking.

• Take the solid light-blue wool and hook a wavy line somewhere in the middle of the ocean area. Choose any of the other four wools and start hooking a line above or below the first line of hooking. Start the second row somewhere near the middle of the first row (not smack dab in the centre; use your intuition here).

• Hook over about seven loops then turn around and start hooking back towards the centre As you do that, start hooking up and down a little instead of straight across

• Continue to so this, switching wools, but sometimes using the same wool two or three times in a row.

• After you have hooked ten or twelve strips of wool, take the variegated yarn and use it

Rolling Waves, 16 by 33 inches.

to hook the horizon line. You can also use a line of navy or black beyond it if you want to accentuate the horizon even more.

• Make sure the royal blue yarn is used all over the ocean area and is balanced out.

• If one strongly coloured yarn is used all over and balanced out you can work the other yarns in more freely, as they will blend together better.

TIPS FOR ENHANCING THIS METHOD

• Change your colours. Colours reflect the time of day, the feeling, the mood, the weather, so by changing your colours you can completely change the look of the ocean. Think about what four colours you would use for a briny ocean coast, Caribbean sea, Pacific waters, Bay of Fundy, stormy seas.

• Go to your wool stash and pull out four wools suitable for hooking some of the oceans mentioned above.

• Add more wools to this mix. You can start by adding one or two more, but then gradually increase them.

• I save the leftover mixes from one ocean rug and use it as a starter for another ocean rug by adding significant amount of new wools to it. This is kind of like making soup and adding to it from day to day: it will be tasty for a while, but after a few meals it might be time for a fresh batch.

• Try adding cream wools, or pale yellow or light grey for the waves. This will give the feeling of movement.

• Try using some really interesting textures in this mix. Add a sweater or mohair scarf to really up the textured quality of the sea.

Hooking Free-form for Movement

My foray into this type of rug began in a different medium altogether. I had purchased an enormous canvas and wanted to try my hand at painting. When I began painting on it, I did a realistic village scene that was a lot like many rugs I had hooked. With the paint, though, I could not achieve the effects I wanted. Everything was blending together and I did not have control over colour and line the way I did when I hooked rugs.

So in an attempt to save the painting I painted it all over in one colour, cream. I liked the way one colour was shining through another, and I like the depth that it achieved. In rug hooking you work with colour beside colour to create movement and shading, so layering and watching colour filter through in a painting was really interesting. As I kept layering I started to love the way red looked on the canvas on top of everything and so I created a big red abstract. I still have this painting and have hung it in my studio for years as a reminder of how hard it is to paint beautifully. Having it hanging there got me thinking about what it might be like to create a rug of a similar design, using a single colour. One winter morning I decided to lay it on the frame as a very large piece and see what I could make happen with the colour red.

I traced out the shape of the rug on the canvas and I drew the first marks—a semicircular swirl—on the base of the design with a Sharpie. I did not draw on all the lines and swirls I planned to add. I decided to let the hook work that out for me, knowing that if I wanted to I could add new lines later with my Sharpie.

Detail from *Intensity*, 54 by 74 inches.

From there I began hooking red wool on this line and used the same colour for about twenty strips. It is tempting to change colour frequently but I really wanted to establish that first piece of form for the rest of the rug. I knew that every other line was going to move out from this one, so it was important to establish it. Keeping my marker on the frame, I would sometimes draw a series of lines and shapes; other times I would take a new red colour and hook a line to create from. There was no overall design or theme other than colour. It evolved as I hooked.

Over the years I have created about thirty of these free-form, abstract rugs. Some have been more successful than others. I think these have been some of my most beautiful rugs—just one colour, or two or three, or even more, blended together beautifully.

TIPS FOR CREATING SINGLE-COLOUR ABSTRACTS

- You want to think about making marks. Practice by gathering a set of colouring pencils or crayons in similar shades. Fill in a page by making odd shapes of colour. These odd shapes will be your marks.

- A mark can be an ameba shape, a circle, a ring, a square, a solid shape, or an outline. It is essentially a doodle and can be repeated again and again in different parts of the rug.

- Make sure you have lots of different marks. I liken them to a painter's brush strokes. Do not use the same mark throughout the entire rug as it will create a patterned effect. (Unless of course that is what you want.)

- Gather different shades of a single colour of wool. Remember, in any colour there are hundreds, perhaps thousands, of shades to choose from.

- For a pillow top you could use between four and twenty shades, and for a large floor carpet you could use anywhere from twenty to hundreds of shades of the same colour.

- Texture works the same way. You can use as much or as little as you like.

- When you use small amounts of texture in a piece, it becomes a noticeable accent. When you use large amounts of texture, you might find that the smoother wools become the noticeable accents.

- You do not want to throw wool at the canvas randomly. These rugs work better when, as you add a new shade or texture, you try to imagine what the finished piece might look like.

In this type of rug you let your hook create the design. You can take your first step by drawing a line with a marker, but you do not need to. If you want, the line can be made with the hook. You are drawing with the hook and following the line. The wandering line as you hook it creates spaces and areas for you to fill in.

The biggest mistake people make with most designs but especially this form of hooking, is feeling they constantly need to change colours after every strip they hook. This makes their rug stripey or hit and miss, instead of having shape and form. Free-form does not mean no form.

- The important elements of design such as balance and composition still matter. Do not get hung up on them, but consider them.

- Do not constantly change colours or textures. Give each wool or texture its due by deciding how much of it to use where. Constantly changing the colour will make your rug like a hit and miss and it will appear striped. This can be a nice look but it is not the idea with these abstracts.

- Remember to hook loosely enough so that you can blend the wools into each other. If you hook too tightly the wools will look as if they are lying side by side instead of blending together to create a new colour.

- Choose three parts of your rug and hook an irregular-shaped area or strong interesting line in the same shade. This helps you establish a foundation. I do not always do this but I believe it is a good way to start.

- If you are working on a large piece you might decide to throw in a related or contrasting colour in a particular area. It should be a colour that it slightly different from the main body colour. Remember that this colour area will become a focal point and will stand out in the rug.

- There are no wrongs or rights in this type of design, but some things will work better than others, as you will discover through experimentation.

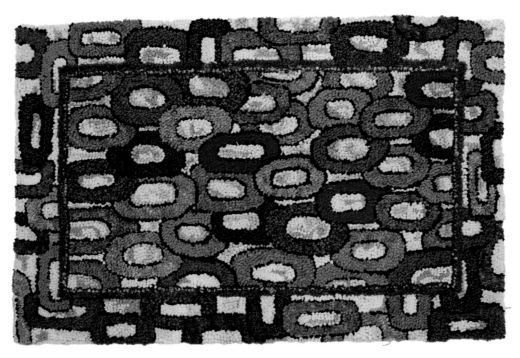

Atlantic Key, 29 by 46 inches.

The Importance of Outlining

Outlining seems so simple when you begin rug hooking. You just outline and fill it in. I loved that when I began hooking because it reminded me of colouring as a child. When I would colour in colouring books I would outline in crayon by pressing it darker, then fill it in by pressing it lightly. When I started hooking rugs it was instinctual for me to hook this way.

When I teach people to hook rugs, I often tell them it is just a matter of outlining and filling in, which is true for a beginner. If, for example, you are hooking a leaf, you will outline the leaf in a darker green, then fill it in with a lighter green. You take the same approach you used to take when you were little with your colouring book and crayons.

Outlining, though, you quickly learn, is very important in rug hooking because it provides a foundation for your design, just like a drawing would for a painting. When you outline you are drawing with wool. For this reason it is important that your outline be more than just a solid heavy line, depending on what you are hooking.

The other tradition in rug hooking is to outline in black or a dark colour. This works well when you want a more primitive look, but there are as many choices for outlining as there are colours.

The style in which you outline, the colour, width, and texture of the cloth or yarn you use will have a big impact on your rug. Over the years I have created some guidelines to help me decide how I should outline a particular rug. Like all my guidelines, I never see them as rules, and know that there are always other possibilities.

TIPS FOR OUTLINING

- Your outline is really a sketch. I often treat my sketch as the outline and I will outline the odd little sketchy marks in my design as well as the main lines because I like the way it holds true to the original drawing.

- Outlining is used to bring attention to a shape or form. The wider the cloth you use, and the stronger the colour, the more attention you will draw to what you are outlining.

- I generally prefer smooth fabrics for outlining.

- The width of the cloth that I use for outlining depends on the size of what I am outlining. If the detail I am working on is tiny I will not outline it. If it is very large then I might use a wider cut for outlining.

- The colour I use for outlining is an important part of the colour plan and I choose it based on the colours I plan to use in the rest of the rug. Your outline colour can also add balance throughout.

- You can use many outline colours in one mat. You do not have to stick to the same outline colour throughout.

- You can use yarns to outline but realize that your outline will be thinner and will recede a bit once the rest of the mat is hooked.

- You can use textured cloths or yarns to outline but because there is so much movement in these fabrics your outline will have less definition.

- I like to outline with solid colours rather than plaids or mottled dyed fabrics because these fabrics change colour and can cause your outline to fade in and out. The purpose of the outline is to make things stand out.

- Deciding when to hook and when not to hook an outline is a personal preference, and requires some artistic intuition. I just use my judgment here, knowing that if I want things to blend then I do not want to outline because an outline separates and distinguishes the item from the rest of the items or the background of the rug.

- The outline is not always a solid line. I often skip lots of holes when I outline. This gives a kind of impressionistic outline that recedes a bit, and though it provides definition it does not make the outlined image appear stiff.

- You can also hook the outline very tightly, packing the cloth so that the outline is more distinguished. I often use this when I include writing in a rug.

- Your outline can be two rows to make it stronger.

- You can also hook your outline higher or lower and this will make it stand out or recede a little.

- You can use the outline to separate the border of a rug from the body. I sometimes use three or four lines of different colours and find that the combination can give your rug a distinctive look.

- Sometimes people like to outline the edges of their rug with a holding line to keep the outside edge of their rug straight. I always recommend taking this line out once the rug is hooked because it creates an odd, thin border that has no purpose in the design.

- There are times when outlining is not required. I generally do not outline in field rugs, the roofs of houses, or faces.

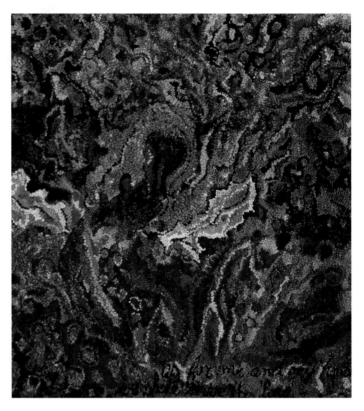

As for me and my house, 54 by 56 inches.

One of the things that makes my rugs unique is the way I outline. I skip lots of spaces and this makes the outline recede a little. There is still a defining line but it does not overtake the image. This makes the rug look a bit more modern than the old-fashioned primitive style of the heavy outline. Your outline is really your foundation sketch in wool. The line matters a lot but it is not meant to be more important or even as important as what it is defining.

Painting with Wool: BLENDING IS THE MOST IMPORTANT LESSON

Sometimes I envy painters. I joke that I often do not introduce myself as an artist because it disappoints people when I tell them that I hook rugs. I kid about it, but there is a certain element of truth there. Painting and sculpture are more recognized as art than rug hooking or any fibre art. This is something I have gotten used to over the years. There has been some progress towards seeing fibre art as "real" art, but mostly you see this in the fibre arts movement itself. Still, there is more recognition among galleries and artists than there once was, and fibre arts are no longer considered domestic handiwork.

I have learned that you *can* paint with wool but that there are limitations. There are things that painters can do that we cannot do with the hook and wool. When it comes down to it, these are the three things that I actually envy about painters: First, painters can mix any colour they need right on their palette. They do not need a dye kitchen. Second, painters are able to blend their colours on the canvas, letting

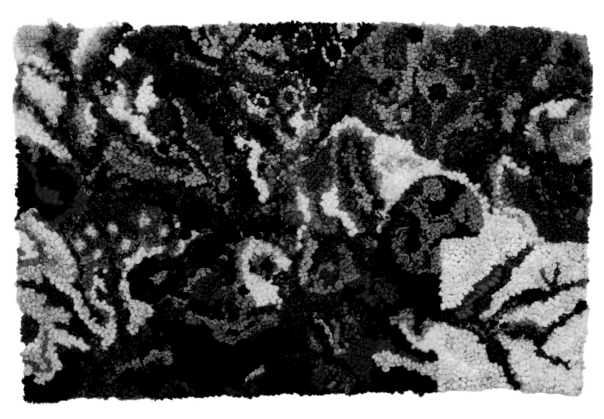

Organic Winter, 22 by 35 inches.

one part of the painting flow into another. Third, painters can layer their colours by painting one colour over another, creating a feeling of light and depth. These three things mean that painters have a great deal of freedom with colour through technique.

The first time I heard the idea of painting with wool, it came from Sylvia MacDonald, a rug-hooking artist from Pictou, Nova Scotia, who made small wall hangings using dyed fleece right off the sheep. Being a longtime rug-hooking teacher with the Rug Hooking Guild of Nova Scotia, Sylvia taught some courses in this and painted with wool herself. She was very comfortable with the idea of using fleece as if it were paint and blending it right in her hooking, and convinced many people that the idea of painting with wool was a good one.

In my work I have played a great deal with wool, and from the beginning I have looked closely at the work of oil and acrylic painters. This research, together with Sylvia's example, has had a lot of influence on my work. I studied painters because I was interested in image and there seems to be an infinite number of images out there. I also studied painters because of the way they make their strokes. Mostly I prefer good quality art books or looking at originals because you can see the kind of strokes the painter uses, and really examine their use of colour.

I find that when I look at an art book I do not look at the overall image as I really do not want to be recreating images that other artists have already seen. Instead I look closely at particular elements that I might try to integrate into my own work. I love to get a big heavy book of a painter I am not so familiar with and get myself a cup of tea and pore over it. You could do the same in a gallery show if you are lucky enough to have the opportunity to see the work live and have lots of time. I do not find that I can really get a good look at the work on a computer screen. The colours are often off and it is difficult to see the textural quality of the paintings, so seeing them in real life, show catalogues, or a good quality book is the best for learning. When I pore over the books I look closely at six things.

COMPOSITION

Where did the artist place the elements of his painting? How far into the painting is the horizon line? What is the focal point or most important element in the painting?

LINE

How did the artist execute the drawing? Where are the main lines? Are the lines soft and organic or hard and defined? How did they divide the painting into area?

FORM AND TEXTURE

What are the main shapes in the painting? How is texture used? Where is the paint thick? Where is it smooth? Why the difference in the same painting? What kind of marks, lines, or strokes are there?

PERSPECTIVE

Does the artist show distance? How are the strokes/lines different when showing something close up and something distant? What is the foreground, middle ground, background? How are they separated from each other?

SKY

If the painting has a sky I always look at the way they treated the sky. What colours and strokes have been used to create the sky? What effect does it have on the mood of the painting? Where is the sun/moon? How did the artist create it?

SPECIFIC ELEMENTS

Trees, houses, people, fields, flowers, whatever you are interested in hooking you will find that artists have painted it. Look at the element and the strokes, lines, and colours that the artist has used to create each one. In doing this you will get ideas about how you could hook similar subject matter.

When I sit with an art book or look at a show in person I study them for these things and learn from them, and slowly over time I add new elements to my own work. They are a great resource for techniques that you can transfer to painting with wool.

When I hook wool I realize that I am making marks and the shape and texture of the marks can easily approximate a brush stroke in painting. You can try this in a small abstract piece if you like. Get out an art book and start recreating the painter's strokes by hooking in strokes on your frame. This approach has given me a lot more control over my hooking and allowed me to create better images. Practice watching out for the way a painter lays down the paint in strokes and use that method in your hooking.

Grey Skies over the Field, 15 by 54 inches.

CHAPTER SEVEN

WOOL DYEING

A s recycled wool became scarcer—with people rarely wearing it anymore and so many more hookers looking for it—I learned about the possibilities of yarn and wool off the bolt. I still prefer recycled wool, but it is often not available. As I became more expressive, I learned that with a simple Crock-Pot from a department store and a packet of dye I could create any colour I wanted. My access to colours and materials became limitless. We have several methods for dyeing wool that we use in the studio. We are often dyeing fairly large quantities and these methods work great for that, but they will also work for smaller quantities of wool.

Summer Bucket Method for Dyeing Wool

Joanna Close has worked at my studio since she was a student at NSCAD. She now is a part-time instructor there after doing her Masters in Textiles at Winchester University in Britain. When my studio was in the house, Joanna worked during the summer looking after the shop and dyeing wool while I took my kids to the shore. It was a beautiful arrangement: she got to dye tons of wool and learn her craft and I got to spend time with my kids on the beach.

I would come back to the studio after a day at the beach and the lawn would be filled with coloured fleece and big green, yellow, and gold swatches of wool would be blowing on the clothesline. It was like something out of a magazine. There was this small, pale, red-headed girl with swathes of wool spread all around my barn and yard. She always looked so pretty there mixing the wools in the steaming dye pots, making colour where there was once only cream fleece.

While walking by Brenda's house, I saw she had her dyed wool hanging out to dry. Brenda works with me and lives just down the road.

Dyeing wool does not have to be complex. Often when people first start to rug hook they feel that dyeing their own wool is an overwhelming idea, and more than one rug hooker, myself included, has said, "I'll never dye wool." Then you learn that in order to make the rugs you want you need to have some control over the colours and you cannot always find the ones you want. But you can always dye the colour you want.

Dyeing wool opens up a whole new aspect of rug hooking and lets you become a bigger part of the process. You can approach it as an exacting craft, measuring the precise amounts of water, dye, and mordant, and keeping records of this to repeat it. You can probably guess from the nature of my work that this is not my approach. I like to dye large quantities of wool at one time so that I have plenty of a colour. I also like to treat wool dyeing as an art in itself, letting the process take over and accepting the dye batch for what comes out.

Throughout those summers Joanna and I discovered that you could dye wool in sunshine in just a bucket of steaming water. We refer to it as the summer bucket method.

SUMMER BUCKET METHOD

- Gather up some large ice cream buckets with lids. You can usually buy them cheaply from stores that sell ice cream by the cone.

- Fill the bucket with a kettle full of boiling water.

- Add your dye. The amount of dye will affect the intensity of the colour.

- Add your wool cloth, fleece, or yarn.

- Put the lid on the bucket and leave it in the sun. The heat of the sun will act like a simmer.

This method is very simple but very effective for dyeing wool without a mess and out in the open air. Even outside, where you do not have to worry about ventilation, it is always a good practice to wear a mask and gloves when you are using wool dyes.

I love pulling the wool out of the dye bath.

- The amount of time you leave the bucket in the sun will also affect the colour. We have tried anywhere from a half an hour to all day.

- Before you take the wool out of the dye bath, add in three tablespoons of citric acid. This will act as a mordant, setting your dye and keeping it from running.

- When you take your wool out of the bucket, put it in a bucket of clean water and rinse it until the wool runs clear and there is no dye left in it.

Washing-Machine Dyeing

Sometimes you find a piece of wool and the colour is too harsh, but the texture or the weight is perfect. Buy it anyway because it is perfect for the dye pot. I save up all these odd bits that I find—colours that are too harsh, an odd piece of silk, an old silk tie, an old blanket, a light plaid skirt—and I add a few yards of other wools off the bolt for a big dye bath in my washing machine.

For this method you need a washing machine that loads from the top, not a front-loader. It is also sensible to wear a mask and gloves to avoid inhaling dyes or getting your hands stained. I try to make a habit of wearing gloves and a mask for the whole process.

You then put as much of the hottest water that your washing machine will allow. When I fill my washing machine with water for an extra large load I can dye up to ten yards of fabric. If you have less wool, then do not fill your washer as high. If you use less water and really pack the wool in tight you will get a more mottled effect. If you want the wool to be more solid than mottled, use lots of water and less wool.

Once the water is in the machine, you can put the dye in and then add your wool. The amount of dye you need depends on how much wool you want to dye and the intensity of the shade you want. For a full load of water I use two tablespoons of dye for a soft lighter shade.

This is a trial and error method and is not good for trying to get an exact shade. It is perfect for dyers who like to experiment. If you start with several different shades and colours, for example a bit of pastel, a bit of gold, some cream, a light plaid, and maybe some light grey, overdyeing them all with one colour will give you a good variety of shades of one colour. This expands your palette quite a bit and gives you a great selection of wool that will work well together in a rug because these materials have been married into the same colour family during the dyeing process.

Once the wool is in the wash with the dye I move the wool around with a pair of tongs. I can then lift the wool out, checking the colours. At this point I can add more dye if I want a deeper colour, or more wool if I have too much dye. You can then let it sit to deepen. Once the wool is the colour I want I then add about four tablespoons of citric acid for a full load and let the washing machine go through its full cycle.

SUGGESTIONS FOR GETTING GOOD RESULTS WITH DYEING

• Add lots of shades and textures of wool to the bath so that you will have lots of colours when it is complete. Add some yellows, creams, greys, tans, pale pinks, whites, if you have them.

• Be sure to use a mordant before you put the machine through its cycle. I use citric acid because it does not smell. You can get it at your local drugstore or wherever you buy your dyes. You can also use vinegar.

• I use many types of dye because there are various shades available from different companies. I do not have strong preferences about dyes—just make sure you choose one that is suitable for wool. (Cushing's and Dharma Trading Co. dyes are the ones we use the most.)

• I used this method in my family washing machine without ever having a problem. My husband has beautiful shirts and they never got dye on them. But the washer can get stained if you are not careful. To be sure, after dyeing you can put the washer through another cycle before you use it again.

• This method is not perfect. It is hard to control the colours you get. It is a method for building your stash of colours. You cannot repeat the shades and dye lots exactly using this method.

• You can dye sweaters, silks, wools, and yarns this way. For yarn, put it in a lingerie bag so it does not get tangled. I leave it skeined and find the twist of the skein sometimes makes the dye more interesting.

• I sometimes use rubber gloves and just dip the yarns in a dye bath for a few minutes, remove them, put them in a bath of citric acid, and rinse them until they run clear. This works too.

• Experiment with colours, mix your dyes to get interesting shades, and play with this method. That is the way you will learn.

BASIC INSTRUCTIONS FOR WASHING-MACHINE DYEING
2 YARDS OF WOOL

- Fill the machine about 1/3 full with hottest water.

- Gather wools. They can be mixed colours and textures.

- Add 1 teaspoon of dye. (I often mix several colours of dye to make a new colour.)

- Put your wool in the water and let sit for 10 minutes covered, then turn off the wash.

- Add 1 cup of vinegar or 2 tablespoons of citric acid and let sit until water clears. Add a little more wool if necessary.

- At this point I sometimes dip in skeins of yarn to dye them lightly, soak up any excess dyes, then toss them in a bath of hot water and vinegar before the wash cycle starts. I rinse these skeins a lot, until they run clear, and get some nice light shades.

- Turn the water to cold, just to save energy, and put the machine through its full cycle.

- Throw the wool in the dryer.

- The dyes might stain the enamel on your machine, so be careful and wipe them up quickly. You can also rinse out your machine by putting it through another cycle.

- Always wear a mask and gloves and follow the directions on your dye containers.

Crock-Pot Dyeing

One of the simplest methods of dyeing wool is by using a Crock-Pot. You can add a bit of water in the Crock-Pot, add your dye and wool, plug it in, and let it sit while you go about your business or hook for an hour. It is essential that once you use the crock pot for dyeing you no longer use it for food consumption (I picked up a Crock-Pot for dyeing at a yard sale for five dollars). Once you've dyed a few skeins of wool, don't go switching it back to stew!

Brenda Clarke does most of the Crock-Pot dyeing at our studio and she has suggested the following method for you to try.

BRENDA CLARKE'S INSTRUCTIONS FOR CROCK-POT DYEING

• First, soak in lukewarm water approximately 1/4 yard of wool fabric or 3 skeins of wool yarn. The wool should be left to soak for about 1 hour.

• Meanwhile, fill a Crock-Pot to half full with warm tap water. (This saves on the time required to heat the water to lukewarm.) Cover and turn the Crock-Pot on high.

• While the pot is heating, mix up the dye solution of your choice with 1 cup of hot water and 1 teaspoon of vinegar. When this is well mixed in a measuring cup pour it into the Crock-Pot and stir.

• Gently squeeze water out of the wool that has been soaking and place the wool in the Crock-Pot. The fabric can be stirred gently and the yarn should be poked down under the water without stirring. Return the lid to the pot.

• As the water heats the dye colour will be absorbed into the wool yarn or fabric. When the water is clear you can turn the pot off and let the contents cool down for a couple of hours.

• When the wool has cooled you can remove it from the pot and rinse well, then hang to dry.

CHAPTER EIGHT

PERSONAL STYLE IS AN EXPLORATION

*Y*ou might not know it yet, but you have a style. We all do. Some of us are born with it...or are we? Some of us seem to have it in one area of our life, and are left to search for it in another. Style is an evolution, an exploration. It develops. As you change it changes with you. It is most importantly about knowing how you like things done and what it is that you like, and pursuing this in every project you take on. I like things loose and casual. I like things to feel natural. I like to be heard. I think all of these things show up in my work.

Self-expression is really just about finding a way to express the interior you. It is a way of showing the world who you are. The mediums for doing this are endless. You could be a writer, dancer, painter, filmmaker, photographer, poet. I am a rug hooker and I have found that this medium is as important a means of self-expression as any other. Traditionally rug hooking has been undervalued. As soon as the rugs were made we wiped the mud off our boots with them. They were left by the door to be worn out. On the one hand this is undervaluing something as art, but on the other hand it is valuing it as utilitarian. Rug hooking is and has always been a utilitarian form of art: we make it and we use it. And so it has had a great deal of value as part of our home and culture.

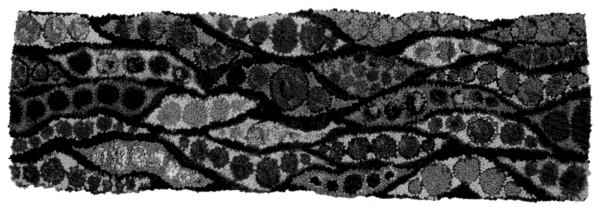

We are Two Peas in a Pod, 17 by 53 inches.

Outside the door was the last stop for hooked rugs in homes. This one, however, *really* hangs on the walls of a home in Ottawa.

It is only in the last twenty years that rug hooking has emerged as a recognized means of self-expression. It always was, of course: as a woman sat by the fire and chose a strip of cloth to hook the sails of her husband's boat, she was telling her story. She was expressing herself, but the utilitarian function of the mat stood out. Today we have the luxury of using the mat not for the floor, but for the walls if we want. Instead being a pastime to while away the hours, we see hooking as a retreat to ourselves, as a way of slowing things down, of holding on to time. Now that our lives have changed so dramatically and we are offered the chance to see rug hooking as a means of self-expression, it matters to us what we hook. We want to hook rugs that reflect our experience, our understanding of ourselves. We want to create something that matters to us. I have hooked my mother more times than I can count. It is rare that I set out to hook a portrait of her. It is just that she keeps emerging as one of the central characters in my rugs. She has broad shoulders, a heavy chest, and is often wearing a bandana. She is the woman I know best, and so when I start to hook a woman she often comes out. I cannot really explain this but I can tell you that like any child I looked at my mother with love day after day, and everything about her sank into me.

Sometimes we find this in a pattern that speaks to us. Sometimes we are drawn to create our own designs. An artist's work is often recognizable. Regardless of the subject matter, there is something that defines their work. It has a certain look, a

I don't sketch enough, and still I have filled at least forty sketchbooks over the years.

certain feel that makes you know just from a glance that it is theirs. Artists struggle with this. I once heard First Nations artist Roger Simon (1954–2000, New Brunswick) interviewed and he said that an artist works very hard to develop a style that is identifiably his and when he does, he is often criticized for that very thing. An artist is criticized because so much of his work looks the same, or feels the same. Yet if an artist is unable to define his own style, he is unable to make his work stand out. Over the years I have really only played with one style of rug hooking, and that has become my own. It just came out of me because I worked at my rugs consistently. It was not something I set out to define. What I do play with, though, is subject matter and design. I remain faithful to the way I like to hook and the materials I like to use. These are the two main elements of my style, and no matter what subject or idea I am working on they remain the essentials of what I am doing. I can look over my work and see different themes: traditionally themed rugs, people, florals, narrative/story rugs, village/community rugs, abstract designs, field/landscape rugs. These are not different styles, rather they are different themes, and my style is built into all of them. My style is just how I like to do things.

What is your style? How do you like to do things? I often hear people tell me they want to loosen up, be more free, let things flow. Then they tell me they are not this way in other areas of their life, or in other types of art/craft that they create. I can show them how I do things, but really I believe their energy would be better spent if they focused on doing things the way they like to do them, rolling with their intuitive style and nature and seeing where this leads them.

Unless you pursue it with your own ideas and intentions, trying to follow a style, whether it belongs to another artist or a clearly defined school of design, goes against the grain of developing your own style. You want to put as much of you into your work as you can fit into it. Think about the following things if you want to develop style.

- What you like.
- What you believe.
- What you deem to be important.
- What you feel sternly about.
- What you find funny.
- What you think is foolish.
- Where you spend your energy.
- Colours that you love.
- Ideas that excite you.

These are the kinds of prompts that you want to consider as you create your own designs. You want to know yourself deeply. Spend time looking at your interior self and with your ideas, and then make art about those ideas.

It is in the time spent making that your style will emerge. You cannot create a defined style in one rug; it emerges over time, over many rugs. In the first few you are just learning, you just make them, often heavily influenced by the style of another artist. You will develop the beginnings of a style in rugs three to twenty. These can be small pieces—remember: not every rug has to be 20 by 30 inches. You can start to develop style working on 5-by-5-inch pieces.

In my own experience, it was around rug twelve or fourteen that I began to see indications of the work I am now doing start to emerge. It was not a straight path from there either. I wavered back and forth, heavily influenced by fashion and the patterns of other rug hookers in the first few years. What *did* stay fast though was doing things the way I liked to do them. I did things that felt right, that made sense to me. I did not look outside of these two things for rules to follow.

Tea and Oranges, 33 by 34 inches.

The only rules that matter in art are the ones you create for yourself because they make the process you are engaged in better for you somehow. Observing them makes your work better. Here is my best advice for those of you who want to develop your own style: Own your own hands. Own your own ideas. Makes lots of rugs and your style will develop.

Claim your space and make it your own.

Speaking with Your Hook: CREATING YOUR PERSONAL STYLE

Creating a personal style can start very early in the learning process of a new craft or art, or it might come later on. It is about defining and following your own path to beauty. It is about knowing what you find to be beautiful. It is about pursuing what you believe to be good taste. It is about knowing yourself and using your art to define it.

For rug hookers personal style is about creating rugs that reflect the world around us and the world inside of us. We need to be intimate with both. So much about personal style is about getting in touch with what you like and reflecting it back to the world. When I first started creating hooked rugs I looked outside of myself for ideas. My first rugs were created because I saw something beautiful in a scrap of wallpaper or in a magazine, and I tried to reflect that. This is a starting point. It is a beginning, and there is no shame in it.

We all start somewhere. The benefit I had of creating rugs inspired by photographs in magazines or paintings or wallpaper was that it was impossible to create the exact same thing as a rug. You could not make a rug look like a picture, so the rug had to define itself. I was working in a different medium from the images that inspired me. I very rarely looked to other rugs as inspiration. This one thing in itself was an important determinant for creating my own style. No matter how much I wanted it to, a hooked rug was not going to look like a photograph. I was going to have to make compromises. There was no way a 1/2-inch strip of wool was going to look like oil paint.

After making about ten rugs, I started thinking about a trip I had taken to outport Newfoundland with my Uncle Donald when I was fifteen. He took my cousin and me across the bay on a small ferry boat to Paradise, Placentia Bay, to a community that had been uprooted during Joey Smallwood's Newfoundland resettlement program in the 1950s. The populations of whole villages on the coast were moved to larger centres that were accessible by road. My father and my uncle had grown up in Paradise, but they were unsentimental about the place having left before the resettlement program. My Uncle Donald said, "I got on the first schooner that came in the harbour when I turned sixteen." My father and his father left in the forties to work at the American Navy base in Argentia, the first time either were ever paid cash for their work. It was reflecting on this visit to Paradise that led me to one style of rug hooking. When I looked back at being on those rolling, rock-filled hills alone with my thoughts it was as if I'd found an element of my story that I did not know I had. This reflection on my trip with my uncle led to the narrative, or storytelling, style that emerged in some of my first rugs. Once I learned to hook rugs my father and mother quickly reminded me that both of their mothers had hooked rugs both as a pastime and out of necessity. I became interested in the personal history of my family and our migration from the outport to Freshwater, just a short boat ride away.

I hook high and with some abandon. It is the way that comes naturally to me. I did not try to cultivate it.

TIPS FOR CREATING YOUR OWN STYLE

- Look outside your medium for inspiration. Instead of looking at other rugs, look at paintings, photographs, et cetera.

- Make friends with your camera. Like a new set of eyes, it will help shape the way you view things.

- When you see something you like, take note in a sketchbook or with a camera.

- Contrasts are a natural element of style. Not every thing you has to reflect sameness. In fact, the things you like can be quite different from each other.

- Change and evolution are important as style develops and morphs over time.

- Review your sketchbook or photos occasionally so that you can see the development of your style.

- Authenticity, being honest about yourself with yourself, is the groundwork for defining style.

Recognizable Style

The work of many artists is highly recognizable. Google some famous artists' names and you will see that with a name comes a style. Modigliani and his gorgeous portraits with the long taupe faces. David Blackwood with his blue-black etchings that tell the story of the Newfoundland outports. Gustav Klimt's portraits of serious, intense faces layered with patterned clothing. We know Van Gogh for his irises and Monet for his water lilies, but it is not so much the image we know as the style that resonates from them. When I think of Alex Colville, photorealist images with a soft cast laid over them come to mind. The style is distinct and clearly the subject matter reflects his voice and experience. He shares what he knows. Another distinct style is true of Christopher Pratt, the Newfoundland artist well known for his hard lines.

If you really look, though, at the work of any artist you will see that they have explored many different ideas in their work, and yet clearly their style comes through. Style is about speaking with an authentic voice, and speaking with an authentic voice is about knowing yourself and confidently putting it forward. All the artists I've mentioned had their own voice, not only in the way they painted, but in the subject matter they reflected. They were all working from an idea, a story, a vision of how they saw things when they created their work. They were not trying to emulate another artist.

When we first start out we emulate. It is the beginning step for many of us. We look to work we like and we try to capture its qualities in our own work. Creating something is a task to be learned. We work to create what we know to be beautiful. It is the first step for many of us. If we look closely at the early work of many famous artists we will see the influences of other artists. I think, though, unless you are looking inward for your own story, your own ideas, then emulating the work of others will never let you speak for yourself. The novelty of creating work just like someone else's will wear off, but the journey of telling your own story, following your own vision, is like a maze you'll never want to get out of. What makes your work speak of you? is a question that not enough people who play with art ask themselves.

Oftentimes we are so interested in learning how someone else creates their work that we are willing to follow a set of instructions so we can create work that looks like that. Many art courses in painting, mixed media, rug hooking, and other crafts are based on this model. The instructor will give you a set of steps, and if you follow them step by step you will learn how to create a particular image. It is a good model for learning, but you must take it with a grain of salt if you want to become an artist. An artist takes lessons like these so that they can learn technique, then they change all the rules of that technique when they bring it to their own work.

As rug hookers, our techniques are like that of an oil painter in that we can create a variety of strokes by hooking our wool in different directions. But in some ways, unlike an oil painter, your tools are limited. You cannot take a comb from your dresser drawer and pull it down the left side of your hooked rug like an oil painter can. You have to search for new methods of discovery in materials that you use, the embellishments you add, the motion of your hook, the story you tell, the subject matter you choose, and the colours you use to express any of these things.

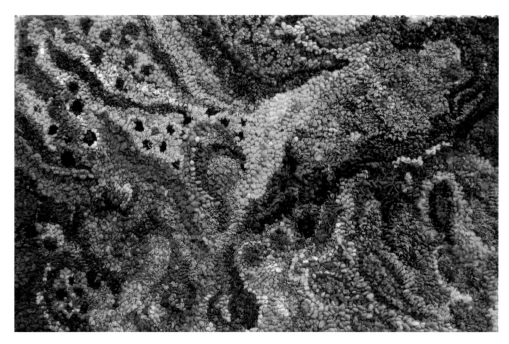

Organic Garden, 22 by 35 inches.

You learn to play with ideas and materials, turn things inside out and upside down and work with them until you are using them in your own way. It sounds so easy but it is hard because you risk so much time and energy. As you push yourself in new directions you make work that is not as beautiful as you set out to make. It is the reality of making art: if you explore you will make mistakes; there will be compromises.

I was always impressed with the painter Nancy Edell (1942–2005). Not satisfied in either medium, she blended painting and rug hooking together. By taking her artwork and adding rug hooking to it, she pushed the boundaries of both and gained some acceptance in the art world for rug hooking and craft as a medium for art. Her work is distinctly Nancy Edell, there is no mistaking it. That is style: when you look at the work and the person's name comes to mind, or when you think of a person's name and their work comes to mind.

Style is indefinable and it is perfectly definable. What the heck does that mean? It means that you could use a million different words to describe a person's style and still not really accurately describe it, yet it is perfectly definable when you see it. Style is found in all types of art. It is about speaking in your own authentic voice. I believe it is about finding what you are good at and being as good at it as you can be. For some people, this is easy. They come across it early and pursue it endlessly. Others need to seek more, work more, before their style develops. I do know, though, that even artists whose very authentic styles shine through in their art still work at it. They work at the creation and development of their style by being as authentic and true to themselves as they can be. When you do this, and you create directly from your heart and bring beauty into the world, you are being of service.

Activity: **DEFINING YOUR STYLE**

As you answer these questions in your journal think about your whole life, not just your hooked rugs, the way you dress, or your home. Try to think of your whole lifestyle.

- What is the one thing you do or create now that your friends and family see as "you"? If you do not know, ask them.

  I am inspired when...
  I feel happy when...
  I feel peaceful when...
  My favourite flower is...
  My favourite book is...
  My favourite outfit is...
  My favourite scent is...
  My best day trip is...
  My favourite word is...
  My best skill is...
  I like to relax by...
  My favourite colour is...
  I love the feel of...

- Do you like clean lines or curvy lines?

- What are the most common colours used around your house? How do they make you feel?

- Do you go for patterns, florals, geometric shapes, stripes?

- What was your style like in your teens, twenties, thirties, forties, fifties, sixties, seventies?

- What elements of your style have remained the same? What things have changed?

- How would you describe your style? Do you like things matchy-matchy or are you a little bit funky? Pick a few words and then explain why you chose them. Try some of these ones if you like: subtle, vivid, playful, random, eccentric, sweet, pretty, flirty, comfortable, feminine, sporty, luxurious, sexy, sophisticated, interesting, plain, romantic, chic, folksy. Look through the dictionary or thesaurus and find more words that reflect you. Write them in your journal.

- Is there a difference between what you are attracted to and what you actually purchase?

- Is there a style you are attracted to but that you don't feel fits you? What is holding you back from adopting that style?

Activity: STYLE BY WORDS

Go through the rugs you have made and then look at the other things you have made, anything that has been handmade by you. Describe the style of each of these things (or a selection of them) using several words for each one. Is there already a style emerging in your work? If so, what is it? Is it the style you want to stick with?

Style-builder Activity: SKETCHING

Take out a fresh sketchbook, or section off an area of one you have, and start designing some simple rugs based on things you are interested in. Draw freely and quickly, not worrying about what the drawings look like. Make fast sketches or thumbnails, perhaps giving yourself a minute for each one or taking lots of time if that's what you need. Take notice of the process that works for you. Start noticing how you work, and how you like to work.

Thumbnails are just small, quick sketches (see p. 28), so do not be intimidated. Just draw as best you can whatever your skills are. Remember, design is not about drawing. Your sketches can be very rough and you can still get a great concept worked out. Have fun with this activity.

Look back at the "Defining your Style" activity (p. 95) and base your sketches on your answers there.

We all have our favourite words, and these are a good place to start when making a word rug.

CHAPTER NINE

SEEKING INSPIRATION
IN THE WORK OF OTHER ARTISTS

*I*t would be nice to think that all our inspiration comes from some deep well inside of us, and that we only influence ourselves. For years folk art, or outsider art, had that feel to it. People worked remotely in rural communities without ever being influenced by the work of other artists. This rarely happens anymore. We are influenced by media and the Internet. There are very few people who can remain outside of these influences. This we need to accept and acknowledge. Art builds upon art. Artists, writers, musicians, and painters have a long history of "stealing" from each other. (In fact there is a book about creativity, published in 2012, titled *Steal Like an Artist* by Austin Kleon.) As artists, we have trained our eyes to really see, to capture beauty, to remember it. We are always on the lookout for a good idea.

Modern Circles on Antique Rocker.

The important thing I believe is that if you want to "steal like an artist" you need to reinvent what you steal and make it your own. Now this does not mean it is okay to copy a picture, change four details, and call it your own design. You need to translate everything you see into your own language. You need to reinterpret it through your own lens. You need to bring your experiences, your vision, and your influences to what you see and recreate it as your own. This is more than changing a bunch of details. This is taking something in, living with it, and reinterpreting it. It is also very important to acknowledge the influences in your work, giving other artists credit if the influences are distinct.

Years ago when I read Natalie Goldberg's book *Writing Down the Bones*, I learned something about imitating style. She told a story about a student who said that every time she went to write she tried to write like a famous writer whose style she admired. Natalie explained to her that it was better to imitate a good writer than it was to imitate someone who could not write at all. It is a natural part of developing style to imitate another artist for a while. Part of learning what you like is seeing what you like, and trying to emulate it. You do not have to do it forever but it is a place to start.

I have been influenced by many artists over the years. Instead of taking a painting and recreating it as a rug, I like to play with the same themes or palettes an artist uses. The advantage we have in rug hooking is that our medium is so different from the medium many artists use that we cannot help but be different when we reinterpret. But the medium itself is not enough of a differentiator; we need to clarify our own vision, acknowledge our own influences, know our own skills and abilities and use them as best as we are able.

As I have become a more established artist I have seen many rug hookers create designs that are similar to mine. When they are hooking my patterns, this is to be expected. There is a long tradition of patterns in rug hooking and it makes a great deal of sense for lots of people who are not interested in designing. When I see people creating their own designs that are very much like mine I just hope they will grow in their art as they continue to design and that I will see their work develop into something that is clearly their own.

As you develop your own design sense it is good to know about other people's art because the inspiration that you get from looking at the work of other artists will teach you a great deal. I love to pore through art books. I rarely read the commentaries unless they are written by the artist. Mostly I just pore over the pictures. I look at how the artist showed movement, what composition they created, their palette. I don't want to recreate what they made, but I like to understand the mechanics of how they expressed themselves.

Let's just say it is hard to create a rug of a starry night without remembering Van Gogh. William Kurelek has captivated Canadians already with his paintings of rural life and Maud Lewis knows black cats. Andrew Wyeth has already captured the man walking across the field. Jackson Pollock has covered the wild strokes of the abstract. David Blackwood has seen resettlement in Newfoundland. Mary Cassatt understands the feeling between mother and child. Lucian Freud has shown us what it is to be alone. So if this is the case does that mean that there is no point in exploring these themes or ideas in our own artwork?

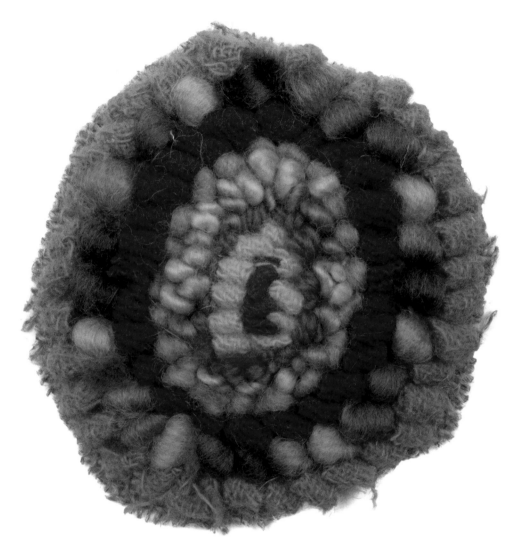

Circle Sampler.

Of course not. Themes and ideas are not owned. There is no copyright on a seascape. No artist owns an idea. What they own is the way that they explore the idea, and the images they create. If you have ever read Ecclesiastes, that beautiful book in the Bible, you will know the verse about how everything under the sun has been done before. We are here to do it again. The real key, though, is doing it again with your own unique vision. Whether it is a lesson in life or re-exploring a theme in art, we are here to do it all over again in our own unique way.

I enjoy looking through the notebooks of Leonardo da Vinci because they show what a diverse artist he was. He played with so many types of art. He was interested in drawing, architecture, sculpture, and engineering. He seemed to have an insatiable curiosity. In his early working life he was not only an artist, but also acted as court organizer for Ludovico Sforza, ruler of Milan. He organized parades, designed costumes, and was a musician and storyteller. He also designed weaponry for Sforza. Da Vinci always had a notebook with him. This is a skill in itself. If one always had pen and paper at one's side so many ideas would be documented instead of lost to us. Da Vinci was not formally educated yet he wrote on philosophy, morality, ethics, and countless other subjects. He drew constantly. When he died in 1519 at the age of sixty-seven he left behind five thousand pages of notes for his assistant. Undoubtedly these notes are responsible for some of the fame he has received. The thing is, there is only one Leonardo da Vinci, but it is also true that there is only one you, there is only one me, there is only one of any of us, and what we think, believe, and want to express matters enough to keep a note of it.

Activity: STYLE INVENTORY

As you go about creating some new rugs, think about how you hook. Make an inventory of the characteristics that relate to your style. In your journal make some notes about the following things in your hooking:

- Are there certain types of wool that you prefer to use consistently?

- Are you a purist about anything in your rug hooking?

- Have you created any rules for yourself that you are consistent about?

- How wide are your cuts of wool?

- Do you have a preferred method of binding?

- Do you have certain strokes or marks in your hooking that you use repeatedly?

- Are you attracted to certain themes in your hooking designs?

- Which rugs have you already hooked that you feel really reflect you?

- How high do you pull your loops?

- What colours do you find you are attracted to repeatedly?

These are practical considerations that might help you define the way you like to hook, which will also help you discover your style. Style being hard to define, these things alone will not confirm any style. Rather they add to your total inventory of thoughts and ideas around your style.

Modern Rug-Hooking Artists and Their Style

LAURA KENNEY

Laura Kenney makes funny rugs. I first met Laura years ago when she came to my studio for a workshop, back when the studio was still in my house. At that time the subjects of her rugs were fairly traditional as she was just learning. Over time, though, I have watched her style develop into something iconic and all her own, and this has mainly to do with her subject matter.

It is not the way Laura hooks or the materials she uses that makes her rugs particularly interesting to me, but more her colour palette, humour, and expressiveness. She identifies herself as a folk artist and agrees that her work is whimsical and playful. She prefers found material and second-hand to new wool, for the story that comes with an old skirt or a pair of pants, and the personality this adds to the wool.

Judy…trying to save a lighthouse, 24 by 15 inches.

Funeral Procession, 38 by 16 inches.

Though she prefers a traditional method of rug hooking using mostly traditional fabrics and a softly primitive palette, Laura's subject matter is quite contemporary. She is completely comfortable expressing her political views or community concerns in a rug. She has been known to carry a large hooked portrait of Prime Minister Stephen Harper to protests. She is also well known for her portrait of a woman on the toilet. Like all good humour, there are layers to Laura's work and lots to discover in each piece. She is clearly intelligent, with strong beliefs, and this emerges clearly in her work, which is both funny and thought-provoking. Art that makes you think and feel is what we all seek, both as viewers and as makers, and Laura's work does both. It is this that makes me consider it a good example of modern design.

Laura believes that we can all make rugs in our own style. She says, "Focus on what you want to say and what you want people to know about you and you will be on the right path."

APRIL DE CONICK

April De Conick was forty years old when she had her son, Alexander. Having hooked for eight years, she left hooking behind to look after Alexander, partly because of the demands of working full time and having children, but partly because she was frustrated with the kind of rugs she was making. She explains: "They just didn't have the colour or style that I could see in my mind's eye. And I wasn't sure how to get it since the kind of colour and style I was interested in achieving was not available in the rug-hooking world. What I wanted to be able to do was paint with wool in an impressionistic style with colour I could control."

In 2007, after moving to Houston, April joined a new guild. Rather than finish up her old projects, she left them stored and started a fresh project that needed colour to flow from one to the next. For this she began to experiment with dyeing and transferred her knowledge of mixing colour from watercolour painting to wool dyeing. She created a unique palette of dye colours from three primary dyes: red, yellow, and blue, eventually winding up with sixty-seven colours dyed in eight values each. This allowed her to create the designs she imagined.

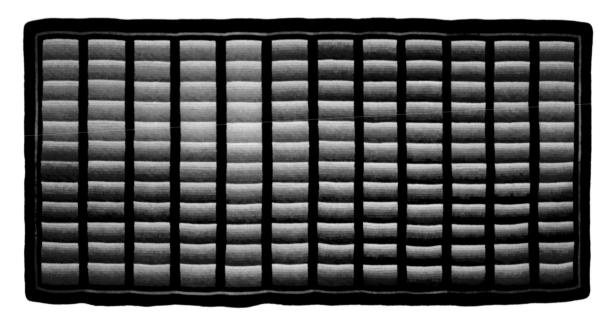

Palette Constellation Rug, 90 by 58 inches. Number 9-cut wool on linen foundation.

Number 6-cut wool on linen. 5 by 5 inches.

April's main interest as an artist is portraiture and scale, and she loves to work both big and small. She draws on her own personal experience and focuses on relationships—the people who make up her life—in her art. April explains, "Even people from the past who I may have never known but who are a part of me and the way I see my world. It is also about animals I have met along the way, creatures who are each just as unique as we are."

For her first rug she did a large portrait of her son. "It was so successful that I knew I had finally found my style, which I call Zonalism. It is an impressionistic style based on hooking zones of value and colour to form the structure of the subject." The style developed by accident when she enlarged a portrait of her son by 400 percent and could see the design as zonal areas of light and dark rather than as facial features like eyes and ears. Using the palette she had dyed she began hooking light and dark zones to create the portrait. When she stepped back from her hooking, the boy smiling back at her was unmistakably her son, Alexander.

She has taken this same method and applied it to many different portraits over the years, feeling much more satisfied and excited by her work than she was before starting over. It was through experimenting that she was able to discover a new style for herself, one that allowed her to express her personal experience and create a beautiful body of meaningful work.

Her work has a modern expressive feel to it that is clearly identifiable as her own. She is also generous about teaching and writing about this style, inviting others to follow her example.

JENNIFER MANUELL

Jennifer has made a lot of beautiful rugs, but the truth is: in the rug-hooking world, she will always be known as The Bag Lady for the incredible purses she makes from hooked rugs. The thing I love about Jennifer's work is that she not only sticks closely to a palette that she loves, she also constructs things impeccably.

Jennifer made her very first purse just before she went to New York City to attend the first hooked-rug day at the American Folk Art Museum, where she wanted to be identifiable as a rug hooker. As Jennifer explained, "That was before I was part of the silver set. I was young for a rug hooker."

When she first learned to rug hook in 1999, the rug-hooking community was bogged down by a lot of rules, technicalities like how high your loops should be. Jennifer explains that if you did not conform you were not really welcome. That has changed of course, in part due to modern rug-hooking artists like Jennifer who believe that modern rug hooking is about not trying to conform to any set of established rules, but trying to do your own thing.

Henry's Pomegranate (2009) was probably the twentieth purse I designed and hooked, and by far it was my favourite. Combining wool strips with sari ribbons and slub yarns made for lots of interest, both during the making and long after it was completed.

Jumbo (Amazing Matrix Mat #5) (2012), is a large, room-sized rug completed over a period of thirty-four weeks. To fill each shape, I tried to cut a bit less of the wool than I would need and supplemented by finding some similar strips in my bins of leftover cut strips. And, yes, it is in use and on the floor!

Jennifer says that she is much more intimidated when she tries to work from others' patterns because when she designs herself she is a bigger part of the process: as soon as she starts putting the pen to the backing she is thinking about the colours and shapes, and she is already involved. Because of this she decided to work exclusively on her own designs.

Her construction methods are flawless and she is a person who thinks of ideas and solutions, so as the ideas kept coming she kept innovating and creating new designs for purses. Her family and friends loved them and eventually she began teaching workshops upon request.

Of course, Jen is more than just a purse maker. She has explored rug hooking from many angles, creating everything from enormous carpets to hooked jewelry. She likes to play with ideas, working them out as she creates. She might use up to fifty different wools in a background.

She dyes her own wool primarily and so has full control over what she is using. Her dye batches cannot be repeated because she does not use recipes; she dyes in her own special way, making her colours unique. She prefers blues, reds, and greens, but forces herself to work in golds too, and knows the important role of neutrals for letting colour shine. She says, "I love colour but colour is not the same thing as bright."

Being a rug hooker is part of Jennifer's identity and she still loves to carry a hooked purse. What she loves most is exploring all shapes and sizes, and feels strongly about following her own ideas rather than someone else's rules. Her work is clearly her own, there is no doubt about that.

Hermiston Zoo (2006), a family game board featuring the ten pets my sister's family had that Christmas. Hooking just one defining feature from each pet greatly sped up the process!

Though I only covered three women here, there are many others who have distinctive and modern styles when it comes to hooking rugs. More and more women are using rug hooking as a medium to express themselves and their own personal style.

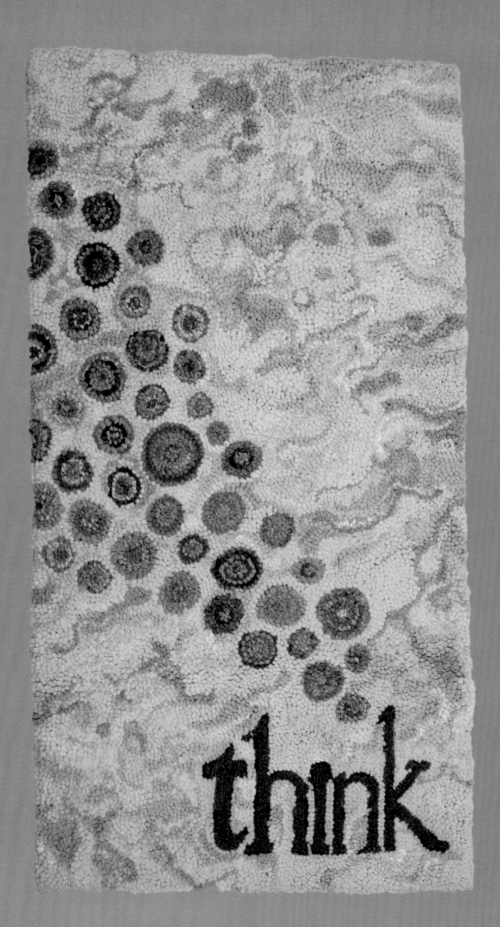

CHAPTER TEN

GETTING CREATIVE WITH RUG-HOOKING PROJECTS

Letters and Words

*S*o much about developing style is being honest. When a person is honest with herself, about herself, and when she chooses to tell the truth as she sees it, style can happen much more naturally. Your style is just you, reflected in your work. That takes some getting to know yourself and your preferences, but rug-hooking is really just reflecting that back.

Words are what we often use to express ourselves, and sometimes to help us understand ourselves. As an exercise, try hooking a word, or maybe two. Choose a word that is important to you; one that feels more uniquely yours than the words we often see written on knick-knacks for sale in gift shops. Think about your word for a bit and come up with something distinctive if you can.

I love words. I love fonts and handwriting and scripts. I remember as a child sitting at a desk where my feet did not hit the floor, swinging my legs and learning the alphabet. I remember being excited. I actually remember thinking that these letters were like blocks and you could make words instead of buildings out of them. I remember

I have hooked the whole alphabet just so I can write words.

how the light was coming in the big windows, a golden orange light that shone on those letters above the chalkboard. I remember being excited to find something new. That feeling came back to me when I started to hook letters to make the sign "create beauty everyday" for my studio window. As soon as I started I realized that I was going to have to write the whole alphabet because there would be other words I would want to write. I would need extra vowels, and a few Ts and Ls. I was transported back to Mrs. Collin's kindergarten classroom. I had gotten ahold of something that was going to open up a new layer of ideas.

The beauty of hooking letters is that you sort of have to follow your own style because your handwriting or printing style takes over and defines what your letters look like. I took the letter project on like this.

- Each letter was its own thing and did not have to look or feel like any other letter in the group because the feeling of the font, my personal printing style, was enough to hold it together.

- Each letter was outlined with a number 8 cut to help define its shape.

- The outline colour led me to choose the colour for the main body of each letter.

- Motifs, such as flowers, polka dots, and stripes, were used on some letters and not others.

- When a letter was a solid colour I mixed a couple of shades to make it interesting.

- A letter hooked in bright plaid will look as if it is mottled because of the nature of a plaid when it is hooked. Using plaid is a simple way of getting several colours in a single letter by only using one wool.

Activity: IN A WORD

Choose a word and create the letters for it. Choose a word that is important to you, colours that reflect your style, and accentuate the letters in a way that you like. Here are a few tips.

- Practice writing the letters in your own hand. I write the letters on the burlap then outline the letter, leaving about 1 1/2 inches of space to fill in with colour.

- Choose a palette that reflects your style and what you find beautiful, perhaps colours that you see already in your home.

- You can decide to outline or not outline the letters. If you outline them, is it one row or two? Is the colour contrasting or does it blend in?

- For the letters, choose embellishments that are your own. You can look at mine, but are there some that would be more you? If so, use them.

- Decorate your letters in your own style.

- To finish your letters, try the glue method I described on page 39.

Speak Your Mind

Years ago when I was studying to be a counsellor, assertiveness training for women was all the rage. It was thought that women needed to be trained to express their thoughts and ideas. Well I would have to say it seems to have worked, because most women now seem to be very good at expressing themselves.

There was a time when we weren't. My mother's generation was much quieter about what they needed and wanted. They kept their cards close to their chest. Today, among many women, expressiveness is seen as a natural right. It is expected that we will be expressive and creative. I suppose this can be daunting if it is not your nature to say what is on your mind, or if perhaps you don't consider yourself creative. Whether you see yourself as expressive and creative, or whether you believe you are not artistic, these hooked-word projects will fit your needs.

I decided that in order to say what I wanted I needed to hook the whole alphabet. (This is my fifth book, so clearly I am one of those people who has a lot to say.) I doubled up on vowels and certain letters. The nice thing, though, is that even if you do not have a lot to say you can just pick a single word and hook it either as a small mat with a background or as a set of letters using the glued method. A set of letters is a great tool for rug hookers. It might be as simple as hooking a child's name or a word that reminds you of something you need more of in your life.

This is my studio and personal motto.
I try to create beauty every day.

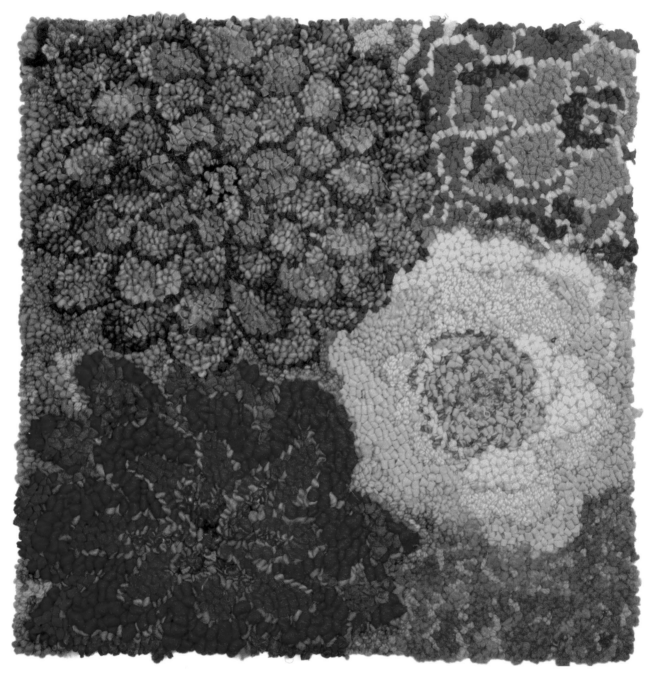

Big Mums, 21 by 21 inches.

Activity: "CHOOSE YOUR WORD" RESOLUTION

Perusing the Internet last year I discovered that many people had abandoned the idea of a New Year's resolution and instead had chosen a word to live by. That is, they picked a word that they wanted more of in their life or a word that reminded them of what they wanted to be; a word that expressed their intention for the year. It might be a word like "knowledge" or "focus" and they will use that word to guide them through the year. You might try choosing a word for your yearly resolution and then hooking it as a reminder to keep your promises to yourself.

Boldness and Florals

When I think of many of the older, traditional hooked rugs they seem kind of meek in many ways. This is partially because the rugs are often quite faded over time and we do not get to see them in their original glory.

Even so, traditional hookers did not have access to the bright colours that we have today with the wide selection of wool dyes and yarn colours. I think there has also been a change in the people making rugs. Today many of us are bolder than we were. We think differently about many things and we are much more comfortable expressing our inner selves than most of our grandmothers were. We are no longer bound by so many traditions and societal rules.

Even when I first started hooking rugs just over twenty years ago, it was a very rule-based craft. There were as many rules for rug hooking as there were for an engineer trying to build a bridge. However, unlike the engineer, the rules for rug hookers were unnecessary. There were rules about the width and height of your loops, the kinds of backing you should use, how you should finish your rug. Many people had taken rug-hooker teacher training from organizations and guilds and were taught to teach in a methodical way, with an emphasis on creating rugs with very even loops, and similar designs being taught in any given class. The goal was to create rugs that looked like your teacher's rather than original, expressive designs.

When I began rug hooking, no one encouraged me to be bold in my designs or to create my own. Truthfully I began creating my own designs because I was frugal and drawing designs on inexpensive burlap was cheaper. But throughout the long history of rug hooking the emphasis has been on hooking patterns. In the late 1800s and early 1900s, peddlers travelled door to door selling pattern designs stamped on burlap. You could also order them from several large mail-order catalogues. Women who could afford it would order their pattern design rather than create their own.

So when I started creating my own designs twenty years ago, often using feed sacks, and hooking with recycled wool, it was bucking a tradition that had been established by guilds and rug-hooking groups through out North America. For some reason I felt it was important to explore the craft as my grandmother might have done. I wanted to use recycled cloth, and I found I liked working with coat-weight wools as well as lighter skirt weights. When I would go to an established rug-hooking group I was seen as "outside the box" even though the traditions I was following were the foundations of rug hooking in Atlantic Canada.

At that time many of the rug hookers I met had come up through the rule-based tradition and felt my methods were a bit unorthodox, to say the least. Being twenty-four and a bit brash, this never bothered me much. I felt I was just approaching rug hooking another way, and that there were lots of right ways to do the same thing. I still feel that way.

I have never really wanted to teach people to hook like me. I want people to hook like themselves, to be free from rules that have no real meaning in their work. I have always taught the importance of being free-spirited and expressive in your approach to rug hooking.

When I think about modern design I think about boldness: a willingness to step outside traditional standards and choose colours and designs that vibrate a freshness that feels new and strong. Having been hooking for over twenty years this is not always easy for me to do. As an established artist you get ensconced in the way you have been doing things and though you have stepped outside the box many times before, over time this can mean you have just created new boxes for yourself. I like to keep pushing myself to explore new ideas. Picasso once said that it was sad to emulate yourself, and I remind myself of this as I try to keep being bold.

One of the ways I have tried to be bolder is in my hooking of floral rugs. In the last couple of years I have gotten very interested in hooking big, strong floral designs that I often refer to as fresh-cut florals. In florals there are so many possible patterns, you can be really inventive with colour and design.

TIPS FOR HOOKING FRESH-CUT FLOWERS

- When you draw your flowers look to the natural world first for your inspiration, but do not feel you have to hold fast to what you find there.

- Look at how designers treat flowers by turning them into motifs. Often a flower from the natural world is turned into a simplified drawing that is really just a reminder of the actual flower itself.

- Draw and sketch lots of flower motifs. Do not worry about each petal looking the same; some can be a little crooked and this will make it look natural.

- When you go to hook them, look at the flowers individually as if each is its own rug or canvas. Work that flower as beautifully as you can before moving to the next. One flower might have several contrasting colours, while another might have only one colour and an outline. There does not have to be a pattern to it, in fact it will work better without one.

- Make sure your flower has lots of area that can be outlined and filled in, allowing the petals and the motif to stand out. I like to make the outline of my flowers quite strong by hooking them fairly close together in a contrasting colour.

I like to build the flowers, outlining and adding the petals. The centres are done either first or last.

- Make sure you contrast the flowers where they butt up against each other, so that a red flower, say, is next to a yellow flower.

- Contrasts can be subtle as well but make sure you can tell one flower from another.

- Every flower need a few accent colours that are close but not so close they get lost in the main colour.

- In the flower centres use rich interesting textures so that they draw the viewer in and give the rug depth. I sometimes just add one loop of a contrasting colour or two loops in different colours. The centre detail is very important. Treat it like a mosaic. Do several layers of outlining. You want to make the centres the jewels of the rug.

- The outlining is important too. In some places hook a single line and in other places double it. This will change the thickness of the line, making the petals appear more natural.

- You can outline in a highly contrasting colour or a subtle contrasting colour. Just make sure that your outline stands out and holds the form of your flower. This is the basis of your design.

Paisley Sky, 8 by 40 inches.

The Textured Landscape and the Paisley Sky

I wrote about hooking the landscape in my previous book, *Inspired Rug-Hooking*, but I wanted to write some more about it here because I believe my landscape rugs are some of my most modern designs. To me when I hang the heavily textured field rugs on the walls, especially the rugs without any houses in them, they appear very contemporary. They remain some of my favourite rugs to make and to look at once they are done.

I am constantly looking at the fields and landscape around me whether I am walking or driving. When I look at the land I see it as series of layers. Starting at the water, next there is the bedrock, then the earth, the grass, the flowers, the bushes, the hills, the trees, the mountains, and the sky. At times I have changed these layers around a bit, or only show a few of them, but in general it is a great way to approach designing and hooking a field or landscape rug. I find that identifying the land like this, in layers, makes me take a playful approach to it.

Each layer becomes an area of space where you can create a design. You can create multiple layer of designs and motifs in each area, or you can pick one or two layers and create a design in those particular areas. I also find that working in layers reminds me to change colours but not too quickly, because when you look at the landscape from a distance it is not stripey but more a series of longer narrow areas.

Fields are particularly intriguing because they are so suited to the medium of hooking rugs. The textures readily available as interesting yarns, dyed or carded

fleece are just crying out to be used as goldenrod, rose bushes, or the scrub along the side of the road. Being a natural fibre, wool takes dyes in very natural-looking shades that mimic the natural seasonal colours of the landscape. Which leads me to the other reason fields are so interesting to hook: because the seasons change here, the colours and textures of the landscape are constantly transforming. Sometimes you can see the changes within the day because of the light, other times it is a touch of frost or heavy rain that might totally transform the side of the road from one day to the next.

I have also played with layering motifs as levels of land in my landscape rugs. This has led to a lot of interesting modern designs for me. This method was inspired by a simple napkin that my sister had at her house. The artist had decorated each element of napkin's lighthouse design with a little motif or mark. It made me see that the lines of my own work created areas that could be approached decoratively. It was one of those "aha" moments that take you to a new place in your work.

I really enjoy looking at the areas of a landscape this way; it gets my imagination rolling thinking of different ways of hooking in the area. Instead of just hooking the layer like I would a traditional landscape, I might hook an area in circles, paisleys, diamonds, or any other shape that comes to mind. I particularly like to use these kinds of designs in the sky and find that doing this transforms the rug into more of a magical scene.

TIPS FOR LAYERING THE LANDSCAPE WITH TEXTURE

• Every material we use is some sort of texture, and the key to using texture well is balancing it throughout the rug.

• I like to contrast one texture with another, so if I use cloth in one area I might butt some fine yarn up against it before using a heavily textured yarn or cloth next to that.

• It is not about constantly changing textures. You can use two or three similar cloths or yarns next to each other for a while before you transition to a completely different texture.

• There can be dramatic changes in colour from one layer to the next, but it is important to keep the same tone in the overall feeling of the rug.

• Flowers can be of a slightly different tone, as they often are in the natural world: you'll sometimes see a little burst of bright yellow or fuchsia in a field that is mostly dull green. Be careful with this, as you can overdo it if you add too many bright spots in a dull field.

• Be brave and use interesting textures, sweaters, fleece right off the sheep, carded fleece, fine yarns, handspun yarns, slub, curly locks, and learn what each can do.

There is a Season, 13 by 16 inches.

Blue Tree Line, 10 by 15 inches.

Blending in the Landscape

In rug hooking you cannot hook one colour on top of another the way you can layer colours in a painting. In rug hooking it is the layering of colour and texture *beside* each other that allows you to blend colour. Because wool is a soft natural fibre, when it is pressured its structure will break down, allowing other colours to blend with it. So when I hook these rugs I hook one area or layer fairly loosely around the edges, then I take another colour or texture and really dig in around the edges, packing the hooking tightly and forcing the colours to blend a bit. This method is important for any kind of blending in rug hooking and it works very well for landscapes.

I also try to hook in very irregular lines and shapes, which leaves me plenty of opportunity to mix in another wool or colour by filling in the odd, irregular spaces with a new colour. Blending your wools is very important in making good landscape rugs. If you look at the natural world you'll see that one colour often seeps into another or completely transforms itself into a new colour. Approximating this in a hooked rug means you have to hook some areas of the rug loosely while you pack the wools in other areas of the rug.

I am careful not to carry wools across the back of the rug. Instead I clip the wool on the top side and start again in another area. Carrying the wool along the back side makes it easy to pull it apart and is not good for the structure of the rug.

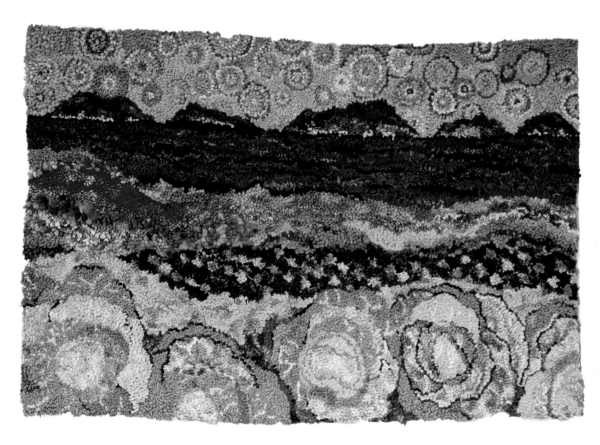

Cabbages, 34 by 52 inches.

Hooking Paisleys

This method is good for paisleys, circles, squares, diamonds, or any other motif and can be used to give a decorative effect to any good-sized area of a rug. Below I will describe how I approach paisleys specifically, but these instructions apply to other motifs as well.

TIPS FOR HOOKING PAISLEYS AND OTHER MOTIFS

• Paisleys are a great motif for the sky, but I have also used them in the ocean and women's clothing. Find the spot you want to decorate and decide upon the motif.

• I draw on the paisleys first, making sure that some are truncated on the edges to achieve a natural look.

• To create an all-over motif it is important that the paisleys reach the edge of the area and not be all centrally located as this affects the overall design. They should cover the entire area you have chosen. Start by putting the first paisley in the middle, then add each one based on the space created around the last one you drew.

- Treat each paisley like a separate work of art. Do not try to make each one exactly the same. Instead, they can be different shapes and sizes. Thinking of each one has unique takes the pressure off as you sketch them out.

- Draw the paisleys on freehand, or use the pattern included in the back of this book as a template. You can copy it onto card stock then cut out the paisleys and trace them onto your backing.

- Pick out a selection of colours that you plan to use for the paisleys. It could be as many colours as you like: twelve, twenty, fifty. I create a palette for them, selecting the wool colours beforehand.

- Make sure you have some contrasts in texture. I like to have some yarns, some handcut cloth, some number 6 cut, and some number 8.

- I also like to have a few odd colours thrown in that are off the general colour scheme because they add a little zest to a few of the paisleys. For example, I might throw a tiny bit of lime in with a bunch of pale blues, but I'll be careful to just use it in a few of the paisleys.

- I often outline all the paisleys first in a variety of colours. You can choose one colour to outline them all in and this will give a nice patterned effect. It will also ensure some colour balance throughout the area.

- As you fill in the paisleys row by row, make sure you take one colour and go all the way around the inside of the outline. Doing this reinforces the shape of the motif and keeps it from getting distorted.

- You can play around with the centres after you have hooked three or four rows of paisley shapes and the shape is very defined. Here you can add some dots or other playful marks.

- You can do one paisley at a time, or you can move around from one paisley to another. Either way can work fine. Be careful not to create a pattern of colour; vary your colour choices as you hook.

- Think about what you might like for a background behind the paisleys. You can choose a single colour, an interesting variegated yarn, or mix several colours.

- The background colour can be in contrast to the paisleys or you can choose a tone that you used in the paisleys and work that into the background for a more subtle contrast.

Not every rug benefits from a paisley sky. Think about whether or not it is the best choice. Will the paisley sky add interest or will it make your rug too busy? Adding paisleys is a design decision and not every rug needs it, so make sure you use it in the right places.

Pillow Power: THE BEGINNINGS OF EXPRESSIONISM

You could say I am just leading you to hook a pillow. Or you could say I am teaching you the power of pillows and their relationship to expressionism. Expressionism means taking a form or idea from nature and changing the lines, abstracting it to some degree, so that it is no longer identifiable but is reminiscent of the original idea. It is a movement in art that started in the early twentieth century as part of modernism, but beyond that is generally considered difficult to define because the approach is often so individualized.

You could say you are beginning to hook abstract rugs or beginning to play with expressionism because that is what these pillows are about. A pillow is the perfect place to start because it is not too daunting.

Choose a size and shape for the pillow that suits your lifestyle, think about where you might put it, and then choose a colour. Take a bunch of shades of one or many colours, keeping in mind that colour evokes feeling and mood. Choose your colours knowing what mood you want to create.

The next thing you might want to do is forget everything you ever learned in rug hooking except the basic stitch. This attempt to create an abstract pillow is really about hooking in every direction with lots of different fabrics. If you want you can draw a few lines on the canvas as a guide for yourself. Just a few simple doodles will get you started. If you are brave enough you could just begin to hook a line or shape on the canvas without any design drawn on. You can choose how you want to approach it.

Summer Flowers pillow, 15 by 15 inches.

You still need to consider the basic rules of design when you hook the pillow. For example you might want a focal point, something that draws the eye. Balancing different shades throughout the pillow top will also make it more pleasing to the eye. One of the simplest mistakes that people tend to make again and again is that they will keep switching colours every time they pick up a new strip of wool. In hooking a small abstract you want to create areas, forms, and shapes of various sizes. This may mean you will hook seven or eight strips of one colour before switching colours. If you constantly switch colours you will be left with a striped or hit-and-miss-style design. This can be very nice but it is more patterned than abstract.

Winterflowers pillow, 15 by 15 inches. Backings are always chosen based on the colours in the pillow.

The lines you hook on this pillow will be your marks, as we discussed in Chapter Three. Making your mark is critical in developing style. This approach is about letting go. Take your hook and begin drawing with wool by hooking lines right on the backing. Hook several lines using your marks you like, whether circles or wavy lines or whatever you like, and then use these lines as a guide to filling in the rest. I like to go around the lines, fill in between them, and make new smaller marks around them.

I find that every mark I make on my pillow with the wool creates a new space around it that has to be defined, outlined, or filled in. You have to think not only about the areas you are creating with your lines but also the spaces that are created *between* your lines. In drawing this is often referred to as the negative space, and it is just as important as the positive space.

Assembling a Hooked Pillow

Hooking pillows has taken off at our studio. People find them easy to create because they are not too large, and they are functional, interesting, and beautiful in a room. I began hooking pillows a few years ago after I hooked the massive red rug called *Intensity*. I loved the idea of hooking one colour in an area, with or without a pattern attached to it. I could just get lost in the hooking without care for what was coming next. It sounds easy, but many people find it hard to create abstract rugs because they find have trouble letting go of their thoughts and following their hands. One of the keys to creating great pillows like these is to forget about what you are doing, let your mind wander, and head towards the zen of hooking. I tell people: close your eyes and pick from the bag of shades—even close your eyes and hook if need be. Stop examining every loop, every strip, and try to imagine the whole thing. It sounds easy, but most people find it difficult.

BASIC INSTRUCTIONS FOR ASSEMBLING A 14-BY-14-INCH SQUARE PILLOW

• With a Sharpie marker, sketch out a basic outline of your design—you can create a series of circles within circles, a paisley design, or a complete abstract—use your imagination!

• Once the pillow top is hooked and pressed, trim the excess backing to within approximately 1 and 1/2 inches from the edge of the hooking.

• Choose a backing that compliments the finished front, such as velvet, wool, or Ultrasuede, keeping in mind that the top and back will be sewn together by hand.

• Measure the hooked area and cut a backing for your pillow that measures approximately 1 inch larger than that.

• Place the two pieces one on top of the other with right sides facing together, then, using straight pins, join the two together on three sides. Using a strong upholstery or quilting thread and a needle, sew the two pieces of fabric together as close to the hooked loops as possible.

• When the pillow is sewn on three sides, turn the pillow right side out and make sure that the backing is not showing around the edge. If the backing shows re-sew with a couple of stitches wherever necessary.

• To stuff the pillow you can either purchase a pillow form that is the right size, or you can purchase loose pillow stuffing and stuff the pillow with small handfuls at a time to avoid lumps. Once the form or stuffing is in the pillow it is then time to sew together the last side.

• To do this, turn the edges of the two pieces to the inside of the pillow and pin together. Then, using thread and needle, carefully sew the two pieces together, closing the pillow. These stitches should be hidden in the fabric as much as possible.

Brenda Clarke proudly wearing a hooked purse.

Joy, a visiting rug hooker, models a carpet bag.

Carpet Bags

When I was a little girl I loved to look in my mother's purse. It was like a chance to get to know her secret life; an invitation to the inner sanctum. Of course there was always a stick of gum in there too (Juicy Fruit or Doublemint usually). I loved rooting around in there, opening and smelling her silver metal tube of lipstick. The purse is a personal thing. We carry our bags with us like a flag really. They show a good deal about us. Some of us have complete offices organized and attached to our shoulders; others just carry the bare necessities. Either way, a bag can be a statement, and most of us love a beautiful statement.

I love to hook rugs, but unlike Jennifer Manuell I am terrible at construction and finishing of such projects. Brenda Clarke and Norma Milner, who work with me at the studio, often help me finish my pillows and bags—or anything that requires much sewing, as I am quite clumsy with finishing techniques. Over the years, though, I have played a lot with the idea of hooked tote bags and for this book decided to hook a few beauties. The hooking for these is the same as the hooking you might do for the pillows, but you could also create a small pattern or design and roll with that to create a really interesting hooked bag.

Handles are always a challenge when you hook a great bag. I have known some people to find a great set of handles on a bag at a thrift store and reuse them. For two of these bags we used standard-style nylon handles from a department store. There are also beautiful custom leather handles available in supply shops.

For the lining in some of these bags I took a picture of the hooking and found a site on the Internet (Spoonflower) and had them create a fabric that was the same pattern as the outside of the bag.

Purses are not really large projects in terms of rug hooking. You can hook the area of the size of the bag you want. They are great for carrying a laptop or an iPad because they are so thick and protective, but they are equally good for lugging around a knitting project and ten lipsticks. Every woman's purse is her own domain. What is important in making a purse is that you make it comfortable and not too heavy. Keep in mind that there is also a lot of finishing work in constructing bags and purses. It is a finicky process, and in order for the bag to feel comfortable and be functional it needs to be finished nicely.

Finishing a Hooked Bag

These instructions are for finishing a rug that has been hooked to an approximate size of 28 inches by 13 inches and is intended to be used as a bag. Also remember this rug will be folded in half, so if you want to do a directional design this must be taken into consideration.

BRENDA CLARKE'S INSTRUCTIONS FOR FINISHING A HOOKED BAG

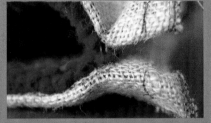

- After the rug has been hooked, serge or zigzag-stitch the backing about 1 and 1/4 inches away from the hooking all the way around to prevent fraying of the backing. Fold the rug in half so that it now measures 13 by 14 inches approximately with the right-hand sides of the hooking together. Using a large-eye wool needle and a yarn that matches the hooking, sew the two sides together making sure to sew very close to the hooking loops directly through the backing. Hand sew the sides together starting at the top, matching the corners very carefully, and work towards the bottom fold. Do both sides. You now have something that looks like a pocket.

- The next thing to do is make a lining. The best fabric to use is one that is light in colour because then you can see into your bag. (Dark linings hide your wallet and lipstick, it seems.) Any fabric will do; it could be cotton, wool, satin. Make a pocket with measurements slightly smaller than the hooked section of the bag. For example, this bag measures 13 by 14 so my lining measurements will be 12 and 1/2 by 13 and 1/2 inches when finished. To make the lining, cut a piece of fabric 28 by 13 inches, fold it in half, and using a 1/4- to 1/2-inch seam allowance, sew the sides together, right sides together, leaving the top open. Do not turn right side out. Set this lining pocket aside for now.

- Next attach the handles of your choice. For our bag we purchased handles and sewed them to the outside of the bag with yarn that matched the hooking.

- Next slip the lining into the cavity of the prepared, hooked portion of the bag. They are now wrong sides together with openings at the top. Fold the top edge of the hooked backing and the top of the lining towards each other and pin carefully around the top of the bag to make sure it is an even fit. Slip stitch the two layers together along the fold line, joining the hooked backing to the lining with heavy thread such as tapestry or quilting thread. By making the stitches quite close together and very close to the hooking, the backing can be completely concealed.

  Your bag is now ready to use. Carry it proudly!

Some small single-colour abstracts framed to look more contemporary than a traditional hooked rug.

Framing Ideas for Modern Designs

I have experimented with many different framing methods for hooked rugs. Mostly I have discovered that it is only smaller rugs that I like framed, though I have seen some of my larger rugs framed after they were purchased and understood that framing has its purposes for larger pieces as well.

There are tons of framing options for hooked rugs, the first of course being no frame at all. Hooked rugs do not need a frame. Once bound by sewing the backing along the back side with a hem stitch, a rug can lie nicely on the wall just as it is and look great. Sometimes people like to hook a solid border around the outside of the rug. This is a very traditional approach and in my mind does not generally look very fresh or modern. I like my rugs just handsewn along the back side and put directly on the wall most of the time. Sometimes, however, playing with frames leads to interesting results.

When I invited April De Conick here as a guest artist in the studio she said that for her hooked rugs she often picks up shadow-box frames in department stores. Flat glass-covered frames do not work that well, but shadow-box frames have the necessary depth.

These shadow-box frames are available now in many different styles, with or without a mat, or with a glass window that opens. If you want to play with this idea just pick up a couple of frames when you are out shopping. When you come home, measure the opening for the frame and create a box exactly that size on your backing. Now the challenge of course will be to fill in that box with an interesting design.

Once you begin to hook, make sure that you hook right on the line, not outside it, making the rug larger than the frame size or smaller than the frame opening size.

Often for my smaller framed pieces I get the frame first and the hook the design to fit it. I sometimes have a carpenter (Brenda's husband Grant, who also makes our Cheticamp frames) create a group of modern-looking frames for me and I make the mats to fit.

Framing rugs takes them to a different place and clearly says that you want them off the floor and on the walls. It elevates them in a way. It is the way in which you frame them, though, that makes them look modern. I like frames with clean, simple lines rather than more traditional styles.

I often decide the framing method before I begin hooking the rug, because this makes them easier to frame.

LETTING GO

A lot of what I do in my rugs is create imaginary places. I make up places and vignettes that I think would be beautiful and joyful and I play with design to create them. For years I have made rugs that I like to call dreamscapes. Wonderful villages with women dancing in the yard and fish jumping in the ocean. They are idyllic. They are the way we imagine life should be.

If you are anything like me, over the years you have come to terms with the fact that the way you imagine life should be and the way it is are quite different. Like our family vacations, when the four of us would pile into the car to go do something as a family only to have all of us tearing our hair out before we even got where we were going. What makes us happy, we've discovered, is to arrive at different times in different vehicles. Mother with one child, father with the other. But as a young mother this is not quite what I had in mind.

Life is what you make it. In real life if you try to stick to imagined ideals you are going to have a hard time finding your joy. It is just the truth. In my rugs, though, I can make my life the way I think it should be. Everyone can live with a rose garden by a seaside cottage. We can all dance in the yard. We can all wave our hands in the air. We can all have glorious overflowing flower boxes. We are limited only by our imagination.

In rug hooking we can imbue a scene with extraordinary beauty with just a few lines and a handful of wool. This is one of the reasons I love it. I can make a little magic and whip up a village. I get to be the creator of someplace beautiful, even if it is only an imaginary place. In this book you will have seen that in my hooking I have moved away from dreamscapes and playful places to finding the joy in simpler designs and patterns. The joy I've found in these has come from sitting with the mat and hooking just for the sake of hooking. The designs became simpler the more I hooked.

For me rug hooking and creating is a kind a prayer. I sit with my hook and slow down. I have no trouble saying or feeling "God." I love that prayer is a part of my life and that I believe there is something out there so much bigger and more powerful than me. I am comfortable with God, and with the idea of God. I know that I need this in my life. Sitting still, taking odd bits and pieces and turning them into something beautiful makes me feel close to God: together we create. I understand not everyone feels this way and that all artists find their own way to create. I just know that when I let go of my desire to control every inch of the design and feel some trust in the process, the rug opens up and unfolds before me.

Letting go of the need to control how things turn out can help you find joy. We have all made a rug that has not worked out. Often we have been so involved in that rug as we made it: We chose wools, tore them out, re-hooked them. We had great plans for it from the very beginning. We had a definite idea and we pursued it with every loop. Loop by loop, we got stiffer and more hunched over.

Imagine instead the rugs you made where you started out with a rough idea and were pleasantly surprised when they were finished. It is not that you were not involved or did not own the project. It is just that you did not try to own the process and instead were willing to let things evolve. In this kind of rug you decided on your basic palette, you found a few pieces to start out, a few pieces turned up in your stash, your friend threw the perfect strand of yarn onto the frame. It came together like a good party.

There needs to be room for something between you and the project and that something is spirit. However you define it, however you find it, however you imagine it, you need to let the spirit into the area between you and your rug and you need to give it lots of room. It is this spirit that will let you feel the joy of making something beautiful.

Robert Henri, the famous painting teacher, said, without the spirit there is no art. Every artist knows that she is not enough, that clearly her work requires her to get out side of herself and let the art spirit flow. So stop pounding yourself. Stop demanding. Stop being so critical. Stop looking for the finish line.

Start again as a beginner with every new rug whenever you can. Start with the joy of making for the sake of making. Only make because you want to make and see what will happen. Do this for a year and watch your work leave the you who wants to control every loop and find a new place inside and outside of you.

Playful ideas are always cropping up. The importance of fooling around with ideas and design cannot be underestimated.

Strengthen your creative energy. Build creative muscle without even trying. Just by making. By shifting one hand over the other, by letting your mind soften, your thoughts roll, the rug itself will no longer be the thing that matters. Instead decide that the process of making it is the thing that matters. I believe that a year of exercising this kind of looseness in your creative decisions will lead you somewhere.

Are you ready? I have no idea, not a clue, where it will lead you. I just trust in the process. When I did this it led to a series of simple modern designs that I never expected. I have learned that making a rug is a process that unfolds. If you persist in trying to make it exactly the way you think it should be, there won't be any room for the process and you'll never let the art of it emerge.

If you compromise a little, give a little, ease up a little, your rugs and your style will evolve the way they are meant to be. Art is a process of emergence. Responding to what happens is the ruby of creativity. Art asks you to become stronger by responding to the mistakes; the things that happen unexpectedly. So as you hook your rugs, start fresh. Start at the beginning. Start like you've never hooked a mat before. Make beauty. Do not make the loop the most important thing. Do not make every colour decision as if it matters too much. Just make it as if it did not matter. Make it as if it were a doormat to be worn down and tattered and lost to generations to come. Make it like you grandmother made it. Make it for the back door.

But mostly, as you make it, make room. Make room for joy. Make room for playfulness. Make room for thankfulness. Make a little room between you and the mat for something larger than yourself. Let there be room for something to happen that is bigger and stronger than you. Make room for your spirit.

Modern Geometric Landscape DF©